D1201049

SAX
APPEAL

SAX APPEAL

Ivy Benson and Her All-Girls Band

JANET TENNANT

ROWMAN & LITTLEFIELD
Lanham • Boulder • New York • London

Published by Rowman & Littlefield
An imprint of The Rowman & Littlefield Publishing Group, Inc.
4501 Forbes Boulevard, Suite 200, Lanham, Maryland 20706
www.rowman.com

Unit A, Whitacre Mews, 26–34 Stannary Street, London SE11 4AB

British Library Cataloguing in Publication Information Available

Library of Congress Cataloging-in-Publication Data
Names: Tennant, Janet, author.
Title: Sax appeal : Ivy Benson and her all-girls band / Janet Tennant.
Description: Lanham : Rowman & Littlefield Publishers, 2020. | Includes
  bibliographical references and index. | Summary: "The story of how Ivy Benson
  rose from a childhood of poverty to become the famous leader of a professional
  all-female jazz band that remained active for over forty years"—Provided by publisher.
Identifiers: LCCN 2020011930 (print) | LCCN 2020011931 (ebook) |
  ISBN 9781538133279 (cloth) | ISBN 9781538133286 (ebook)
Subjects: LCSH: Benson, Ivy, 1913–1993. | Women band directors—England—
  Biography. | Women jazz musicians—England—Biography. | Band directors—
  England—Biography. | Jazz musicians—England—Biography.
Classification: LCC ML422.B396 T46 2020 (print) | LCC ML422.B396 (ebook) |
  DDC 782.42165092/2 [B]—dc23
LC record available at https://lccn.loc.gov/2020011930
LC ebook record available at https://lccn.loc.gov/2020011931

♾™ The paper used in this publication meets the minimum requirements of American
National Standard for Information Sciences—Permanence of Paper for Printed Library
Materials, ANSI/NISO Z39.48-1992

For Keith
With love and thanks

CONTENTS

PREFACE

Just how I first became so interested in the story of Ivy Benson I can't quite remember. Perhaps the unexpected—at least to me—sound of a big jazz band playing at the Proms (the Henry Wood Promenade Concerts) struck a chord. Perhaps it was the increased media coverage of everything wartime when the World War I centenary commemorations started in 2014. Or perhaps it was the coverage of the seventieth anniversary of the end of World War II in 2015. I missed that war. But as a child I well remember listening to *Family Favourites* and *Music While You Work* on our crackly wireless and to my mother, who had a totally off-key voice, joining in the women's vocals. *Family Favourites* was the successor to the wartime show *Forces Favourites* and was broadcast at Sunday lunchtimes on the BBC Light Programme and the British Forces Broadcasting Service. Its exotic-sounding locations and music linking those in Britain to their families serving overseas were a feature of our Sunday lunchtimes for many years. My mother worked shifts, and although the radio didn't play in her noisy factory, I listened with her to *Music While You Work* as she got ready to go to the cotton mill if I was on holiday from school. It was a radio program of continuous live popular music broadcast in the United Kingdom and aired twice daily on workdays. The music was the popular variety, played at an even tempo and aimed to help factory workers become more productive. I remember mostly the dance and brass bands and dancing around to the beat. Ivy Benson and her band appeared frequently on the radio, but as a child I would not have distinguished one band from another by name. But the name *Ivy Benson* must have been deep in my memory and surfaced many years later.

So I had always known of the existence of Ivy Benson and her band, although growing up in the 1950s and 1960s my music was firstly jive, taught by an older sister, and then skiffle, the Beatles, and the Rolling Stones. With the increasing opportunities for women emerging in those days, an all-girls band would have seemed an anachronism to my younger self rather than the example of female emancipation that it would become in the 1970s. But despite not knowing quite why I had become interested in her, I decided, in 2015, to investigate Ivy's story further. I was close to publishing my book on Ursula Vaughan Williams, mistress and second wife of composer Ralph Vaughan Williams, and new research into Ivy Benson's life was an interesting break from final editing. I was hooked on her story.

My research into Ivy Benson over the last few years has coincided with renewed interest in dance band music. Clare Teal's extremely successful band concerts at the summer Proms are an example of how an erstwhile-classical music event has embraced band music. There was also renewed interest in Ivy Benson herself as the centenary of her birth in 1913 came and went. In 2014 and 2015 Melanie C (Chisholm), Sporty Spice of the Spice Girls, hosted two radio programs featuring Ivy as a prime example of a feisty and successful female musician, and I believe there have been at least two academic studies of her—a student essay and an oral-history PhD dissertation.

Ivy Benson was born in comparative poverty in Leeds in 1913. She lived all her life in the twentieth century—a century that encompassed two major wars, a depression, postwar austerity, continuing male chauvinism in the music industry, the phenomenon of the 1960s, and the rise of feminism. With true Yorkshire grit, she both used the opportunities of her century and overcame its difficulties to succeed in a way that no woman had done before.

PROLOGUE

The year—1924. The place—Empire Palace Theatre, Leeds, Yorkshire, England.

The small, auburn-haired girl curtsied to Florrie Forde, the famous music-hall star, before turning to beam at the audience as she received her prize, a dollhouse. She had just sung a comic song to win the children's talent contest at the Leeds Empire that night. The audience clapped enthusiastically as the confident ten-year-old smiled down at them. Ivy Benson was a born performer.

Even at this young age she was known for her musical talent in the city where she lived and was already contributing to the family finances by playing the piano in clubs and pubs. Her father, Douglas "Digger" Benson, himself a good musician, had taught his daughter well. He had plans for Ivy to become a professional pianist. But although she loved playing the piano, Ivy had other ideas.

As a musical child growing up in the 1920s, Ivy would have been surrounded by the big band sound that was the soundtrack to the period. Dance bands could be heard by everyone on the new "wirelesses," and a gramophone or record player had become a part of many households. Determined to be a professional musician, young Ivy was never going to settle for working in a factory, which most girls from her background had to do. And although she had started her working life as a factory clerk, luck and her father's connections intervened. At only fifteen she started her professional life playing the saxophone in an all-women band at a seaside resort on the East Yorkshire coast.

Moving to London in her early twenties, Ivy worked hard, playing gigs in small venues and seedy clubs, but it was not easy for women instrumentalists to break into the almost-totally male bands. An opportunity arose to play lead sax in an all-girl band, conducted by male bandleader Teddy Joyce. The experience was not a particularly good one for Ivy, and she and the other women were dissatisfied with their treatment and their pay. It wasn't what Ivy wanted.

In September 1939, Germany invaded Poland, and three days later Britain declared war on Germany. Suddenly life changed irrevocably for many people in the British Isles; danger, hardship, and separations characterized the next six years. For the young Ivy Benson, however, it was the beginning of a new life. The unique climate created by World War II and its aftermath, Ivy's ambition and preparedness to take any opportunities offered, her sheer bloody-minded determination to fight what she saw as injustice, and just a little luck made her a success in a field known for its capriciousness even if you weren't a woman.

With the onset of the war years, Ivy took her chance, forming her own all-girl swing band with a nucleus of the dissatisfied Teddy Joyce musicians. It was a timely business decision: male instrumentalists were being called up for military service just as demand was increasing for entertainment to maintain morale for both troops and civilians. One of the few male bandleaders who did not resent her, the influential Jack Hylton, opened up opportunities for Ivy and her band, which went on to become extremely popular with both civilian and military audiences. At the height of the war, Ivy was receiving over three hundred letters of appreciation weekly from soldiers, sailors, and airmen.

But it wasn't easy going. In addition to coping with bombings, protecting her young charges, and single-handedly managing the financial and organizational aspects of her business, Ivy faced male opposition and chauvinism from the start.

Throughout the war and well into the postwar period, her band toured widely in the United Kingdom, entertaining troops and civilians. They also played on military bases overseas. Like most of the thousands of recruits to the Entertainments National Service Association—from well-known stars to near amateurs—Ivy and her band traveled constantly to perform for the people, working in a variety of makeshift theaters, where the stage was often just a few tables perched on oil drums. Although her band members were young and glamorous—and magnets to lonely soldiers, airmen, and sailors—Ivy insisted that they were musicians first and foremost and that they play as well as their male counterparts. She was a good coach and a strict taskmaster.

Once again, after the war ended, a combination of political and historical decisions outside her control as well as her own indomitable spirit helped her make decisions that would ensure her continuing success. Ivy and her band, grown accustomed to full employment, seemed to find less and less work as male musicians began returning from service. Even the BBC seemed to turn against her, when, unlike the all-male bands, Ivy's contract was not renewed with the broadcaster. Angry at such treatment, she retaliated, taking her band on their first European tour, to Berlin, to play for Allied troops. This proved to be a turning point in her fortunes, and that visit to Berlin became the first of what would become regular tours postwar, many of them to US bases, which would continue for many years.

This proved to be a wise move, as she developed a loyal fan base that supported her for many years after the war. These tours combined with summer seasons at well-known British seaside resorts became her staple work. There she often worked alongside numerous celebrities of the day and grew to consider many of them friends. In the 1950s and onward she developed her repertoire in line with the rapidly changing music scene and became adept at playing for different audiences.

A problem that never went away, in all her decades as a bandleader, was getting and keeping her performers. During the war years, she wasn't the only bandleader on the lookout for good musicians; but she kept her eyes and ears open for promising young women and was always prepared to train them to the standard she required. "I once took a girl from a pie factory and made her a bass guitarist," she claimed.

Having been born and raised in Yorkshire, Ivy was familiar with the brass band tradition of England's industrial north, where she was helped by her contacts there. She found a particular booster in Harry Mortimer, a specialist in brass band music whom she liked and whose judgment she trusted; he knew of many promising players and over the years sent a stream of them to Ivy for auditions.

Keeping her musicians was even more difficult than finding them in the first place. "I sometimes thought it was not so much a band as a mobile marriage market," she once commented wryly. Over the years, hundreds of women worked for her, and there were always chairs to fill. American servicemen caused her particular problems, as she always seemed to lose women to GIs on her frequent tours to American bases. She herself was not immune to the attractions of the Americans; her second marriage was to a serving American soldier.

Over her forty years of touring and playing, Ivy built up a rich trove of stories of life in a women's band—some sad, many funny. From dodging bombs in London and Manchester, to trying to cheer weeping, lovesick players, to battling the bats, mud, and peeping toms that seemed endemic to military bases, to losing a player to a GI mid-concert—Ivy coped with it all. And this was on top of the danger, horror, and grief of performing in active war zones and in grounds that had only just seen bloodshed and stupefying destruction.

Later in life, Ivy admitted that she had often been worried and upset by the pressures unique to this type of demanding work, but it rarely showed; most of those who worked for her remember a strong character who ran a professional band with high standards. During all four decades she was a bandleader, she always had an all-girl line-up, even though after the Sex Discrimination Act of 1975, she changed the name of her band from Ivy Benson and Her All Girls Band to the Ivy Benson Show Band—and in theory was prepared to employ men, "if they could fit into a size twelve to sixteen stage costume."

Many women musicians have cause to be grateful to Ivy Benson for giving them the chance to play professionally, and in recent years her artistry and pioneering spirit have been increasingly recognized by a new generation of musicians and enthusiasts not yet born when she was making her mark. She has particularly served as a positive role model for women musicians who want to front their own groups and make it in the music business.

"I didn't make a lot of money," Ivy said toward the end of her career, "but the money side came second to making something comparable to the male bands. I don't normally look back, but I like to think I achieved that, and it means a lot to me."

Ivy's story is one well worth the telling.

1

THE BIG BANDS

Late 1935, the Tower Ballroom in Blackpool, a seaside town in the northwest of England. Thousands of people mill around the edges of the room, waiting. Others crowd the gilt upper balconies, eagerly anticipating the music. There is a palpable buzz of excitement. Suddenly, a burst of sound erupts from the stage. Feet start tapping to the swing beat, and couples surge onto the polished-wood dance floor. Onstage, Bertini and the Blackpool Tower Dance Band blast out the music. Saxophones, trombones, and trumpets lead the way: the rhythm section keeps a syncopated beat. The music is mostly jazz with an increasing swing tempo.

Now go to any ballroom, in any town, in any part of Britain. All over the country, it's the same: the people want to dance.

This enthusiasm for the music of big bands was by no means new in mid-1930s England. After the horrors of World War I had begun to recede, young people wanted to enjoy themselves again and began letting their hair down. There was plenty of dance music to listen to, and many bands were touring the country, providing the beat for this urge to dance. Throughout the 1920s, the sounds of American band music had infiltrated British radio broadcasts and records, and the number of British bands had grown exponentially. You didn't have to be in London with money enough to visit the fashionable clubs to enjoy big band music; it was available to all.

There had always been orchestras for dancing, but dance bands and the later so-called big bands owed a great deal to the early ragtime bands in America. Big band music was increasingly syncopated, developed from ragtime and embellished by jazz musicians. Before 1912 such bands usually had a violin taking the lead, backed by piano, drums, and a banjo. But as more printed music became available, with clearly defined parts, the number of musicians grew, and the accepted instrumentation became two or more brass, plus a rhythm section of piano, banjo, drums, and bass brass (string bass would come later). Sometimes the violin was retained.

The popularity of dance music and later big band music in the 1920s was owing to mainly three things: touring and personal appearances by the great bands, the very successful sales of gramophones, and regular radio broadcasts. By 1921 the gramophone had become a mass medium capable of providing artists with an audience of hundreds of thousands—and those audiences with almost-instantaneous exposure to the newest music. Sheet music too, despite a decline in sales, was important in changing people's home music from Victorian and music hall ballads to dance tunes. Dominating this period were publishers like Lawrence Wright and Chappell (later Warner Chappell Music), who took out large advertisements in the trade and national press for their piano scores, along with popular tunes of the day, arranged in a number of ways and for different sizes of group or orchestras. Everybody could thus hear the same arrangement on record, and later on radio, but local dance bands could also play the same tune in the same way as the famous bands of the time. Dance music was further promoted by additions to the gramophone trade press, including the monthly *Gramophone* and the weekly *Melody Maker*. All three influences—personal appearances, gramophone records, and national radio broadcasts—were interconnected, each boosting the other. Links with local radio stations were crucial too, often leading to sponsors contracting the bands for nationwide (network) shows. Such a career path was best exemplified by that of American bandleader Paul Whiteman, who was extremely popular during the 1920s. His first record, the single "Wang-Wang Blues," sold 457,000 copies worldwide in 1920, while his disc featuring "Whispering" and "Japanese Sandman" sold over one million copies in Britain. Whiteman had nine hit records in 1921 alone. Championing symphonic syncopation, Whitehead popularized a style of arrangement that became a major influence on British dance bands. Unlike the music of novelty bands, Whitehead's pieces were carefully arranged, rather than the parts emerging haphazardly between musicians in practice sessions. Instead, this new kind of instrumentation was conceived as a replicable whole by the arranger, who also set out the soloists' parts, including their improvisations, creating a piece that was replicable.

During a visit to Britain in 1923, Whitman gave a performance seen by British bandleader Jack Payne. "Here, I thought, was a real show band," recalled Payne, impressed by the American's orchestrations and showmanship. "Whiteman didn't just play; he presented his band as a stage entertainment. I have never forgotten the deep impression which that difference made on me. I decided that as soon as ever I had the chance, I would feature my band just that way." Which he did when, in 1925, Payne went on to play in the house band at London's Hotel Cecil.

Indeed, the most important task of any aspiring bandleader of the day was to secure just such a "shop-window" engagement—a residency at one of the grand hotels, clubs, or restaurants. From there, other forms of media—recording, radio, theater—would bring national popularity within reach. And it never hurt to take musical cues from the trendsetters. As Whiteman's work moved closer to light orchestral music, especially his use of strings, British bands, including the Savoy Orpheans, Jack Hylton's band, and Jack Payne's BBC Dance Orchestra, soon followed his lead. These lush arrangements, with their steady tempo and smooth solos, were preferred by glamorous couples dancing in the most exclusive hotel ballrooms, restaurant dance floors, and nightclubs. After a Whiteman performance at Manhattan's Aeolian Hall in January 1925, the Savoy Havana Band combined with the Savoy Orpheans to put on a concert of "symphonic syncopation" at the Queens Hall in London, and it was after Whiteman's band featuring "hot" soloists, like Bix Beiderbecke, that British bands began to allow their own soloists to play "hotter."

Whiteman was by no means the only big band leader in the 1920s, but he was the most successful and publicized. By a stroke of luck, in 1920 he was leading a band playing the opening of the Ambassador Hotel in Atlantic City where the Victor Talking Machine Company happened to be holding its annual convention. This chance meeting led to "Whispering," the first-ever record to achieve over a million sales. Whiteman played to the rich and famous of that generation, such as the Vanderbilts, one of America's wealthiest and most influential families, and Lord and Lady Mountbatten danced to his tunes during a visit from England. Whiteman was immensely successful. Although after the advent of swing his band began to sound a little dated, his success and the publicity he gave to dance music were outstanding features of the 1920s. Bands proliferated throughout America, many of them jazz-orientated, playing big band versions of jazz classics.

Often, big band addicts minimize the importance of the so-called "sweet" bands, which also got their start in the 1920s. These smaller, more conventional dance bands usually were comprised of five to ten musicians playing a repertoire that was more lyrical than syncopated and that included more ballads. Guy Lombardo, with his band the Royal Canadians, best exemplify this popular style; he claimed to play "the sweetest music this side of Heaven." Although Lombardo's sweet big band music was viewed by some in the jazz and big band community of the day as "boring, mainstream pap," trumpeter Louis Armstrong was no such critic. Even though he led a jazz band, Armstrong told reporters that he and his band listened to Lombardo as long as his Saturday-night program *The Owl Club* aired.

As well as the mostly white, jazz-based, big bands and the sweet bands, the black bands that managed to break through the color-prejudice barrier to some degree were key to shaping the big band scene in America. Fletcher Henderson led one of the earliest of these, when he arrived in New York from Georgia in 1920. A talented pianist, arranger, and composer, by 1924 Henderson and his band were resident at Roseland Ballroom, a post they kept for ten years. He eventually gave up the band due to various vicissitudes but not before nurturing many talented musicians, including Coleman Hawkins and Don Redman, and hosting other passing greats, including Louis Armstrong. But though black bands played extensively in clubs and theaters, they were hardly ever booked to play ballrooms or hotels for dancing. And so it is truly ironic that it was Fletcher Henderson's arrangement of "King Porter Stomp," played by the band of Benny Goodman, that is generally thought to have started the swing era. Of that, more later.

The most remarkable and long-lasting career of a black band-leader was that of Edward Kennedy "Duke" Ellington. He and Elmer Snowden formed a band, the Washingtonians, and in 1923 were engaged at the Hollywood Club in New York, with Snowden leading and Duke on piano. This arrangement was soon reversed, however, and by 1924 Duke was leading and Snowden backing in the band. The band's big break came in 1925 when it secured a seven-year residency at the Cotton Club in Harlem, which, in its heyday, was the most famous entertainment venue in the world, featuring alongside the Ellington band singers such as Ethel Waters and Lena Horne. During their Cotton Club residency Ellington's band recorded their music in a small way as early as 1925, but after 1931 their output was legendary.

But if the stars at the Cotton Club were black, most of the audience was white. During their time at the club, Ellington's band took leave for extensive tours in America, and in 1933 they toured Britain and France. There, as in the United States, they played almost entirely in theaters, since black players were still separated from their audiences due to an unofficial but active color bar. It could be said that Duke Ellington's band was not fully accepted by white audiences, other than ardent jazz fans, until many years later when, in 1943, he appeared at Carnegie Hall. Asked on one occasion how he felt about the fact that even in the 1930s his and other black bands were not welcome in America's hotels, restaurants, and ballrooms, the wonderfully pragmatic, always urbane Ellington replied, "I took the energy it takes to pout and wrote some blues."

However, during the early 1930s, few changes in the big band scene would have been noticeable to those who had followed the music from the 1920s. Big bands, sweet bands, and the jazz-orientated black bands continued to provide the music of a generation. Some historians believe that the Wall Street stock market crash of 1929 and ensuing Great Depression increased a desire for "sweet" music, but Mark White argues that, although some bands did fall by the wayside in this period, other similar groups in all three spheres of band music quickly took their place.

Across the ocean, Britain also enjoyed its share of big bands. However, they did not slot as easily into style categories as did their American counterparts; there was not the same jazz tradition in Britain and neither was there the element of black music. The best of these big bands played in London, at extravagant hotels like the May Fair—and also the legendary Savoy. One of the earliest venues for dance music, the Savoy had catered to dancing since World War I, and by 1921 the Savoy Havana Band, led by American saxophonist Bert Ralton, was the resident band. When Ralton left for Australia in 1923, the Savoy Orpheans, led by Debroy Somers, took the lead, supported by the Havana Band, now under the leadership of Reg Batten. Although no one American band alone could be said to have been the principal influence on British musicians, many bands did visit, including Paul Whiteman's, inevitably leaving their mark. In 1922, The Savoy in London created a stir by engaging the Savoy Havana Band led by American saxophonist Bert Ralton. In 1923 Paul Whiteman and his band played to a society clientele at the Grafton Galleries in London. From this time up to the start of World War II, many American bands and instrumentalists came to Britain, staying for varying periods of time. Perhaps one of the strongest contributors to the increasingly jazzy sound of British dance music was Spanish-American pianist Fred Elizalde, who, in 1927, was invited to take a band of jazz musicians to the Savoy ballroom to play opposite the famous Orpheans.

In Britain, as in America, bands playing the prestige venues were comprised entirely of male musicians and led by charismatic male bandleaders, all with their individual styles and recognizable theme tunes. These bandleaders were the pop stars of the era, earning big money and living visibly lavish lifestyles, which were eagerly detailed in magazines and periodicals of the day, including *Time Life* and *Vanity Fair*, forerunners to Britain's celebrity magazines of today, such as *Hello!* and *Heat*.

One of these early, well-known bandleaders was Bert Ambrose, a fixture in London's West End, who played for high-society audiences. Born in London in 1897, Ambrose was raised in the United States, having emigrated with his family when he was a schoolboy. But in 1920, at twenty-three, he moved back to London to front a quintet and serve as musical director at the Embassy Club. He soon returned to the States with the intention of recruiting musicians for his London group, but the draw of playing at New York's Clover Gardens was too strong an attraction, and it was some time before he returned to London with many of his best musicians, to a seven-year residency at the May Fair Hotel. Once reestablished in Britain, he and his band became great favorites of the royal family and often played at Windsor and Buckingham Palace. Ambrose's band broadcast from the May Fair every Saturday night, solidifying his popularity nationally. After the May Fair, he moved on to the Embassy Club, then Ciro's, then Café de Paris. In the summer Ambrose would play at upscale continental resorts such as the Monte Carlo Casino, where he could indulge in his love of gambling. Everyone wanted to play for him: he paid the highest wages and was known for only hiring the best. A spell with him almost guaranteed future employment.

But there were plenty of homegrown bands in Britain too, and while the best of them gravitated to London, many bands—numerous if less well-known—toured the countryside to play in concert and dance halls for ordinary folk. One of the most important and influential bandleaders of 1920s Britain—and important to our ongoing story—was Jack Hylton. Born in Bolton, Lancashire, Hylton moved to London in 1913 where he played various clubs as a pianist, until spending the war years in the entertainment division of the Army. In 1920 he became a pianist with the Queen's Hall Roof Orchestra, and by 1921 he was already making records. Intentionally or not, Hylton's professional rise seemed to be modeled on the career trajectory of Paul Whiteman.

Hylton attracted excellent musicians to his payroll, including tenor saxophonist Billy Ternent, who would later become the band's arranger and go on to lead one of Britain's best-known orchestras. Ternent, too, in a different way than Hylton, would have a bearing on Ivy Benson's story and her battle for acceptance as a bandleader and for the appreciation of the quality of her women musicians.

Some time around 1926, Hylton gave up his policy of playing straightforward dance music and set out to create what we would call a "showband." He and his band toured the theaters of Britain, specializing in big entertainment numbers that combined music with spectacle. According to one story, the band played before an elaborate desert set, designed for their interpretation of the popular song of the time "Sahara": every night, the singer would arrive onstage dressed as a sheik, styled after silver-screen heartthrob Rudolph Valentino in his 1926 film *The Sheik*, and riding a live camel. One night, the camel, not having been given the chance to relieve itself before its entry, did so backstage just before its cue and fused the footlights, plunging the stage into darkness.

Despite Hylton's success in Britain, his attempts to present the band in America failed. American unions protected their own performers from incursion by foreign bands, and in 1929 a strike was threatened by the pit musicians at New York's Paramount Theatre when Hylton was engaged to play there. And again, in 1935, he was barred from playing by the American Federation of Musicians. Individually, however, Hylton and his musicians did share the stage with American players, and some of his specialty acts were performed. A real entrepreneur, Hylton arranged tours in mainland Europe too and became a director and major shareholder of the new Decca record label. He became a wealthy man but spent lavishly.

Perhaps one more bandleader of the very many is worth mentioning at this stage for his impact on Britain's listening habits. In 1928 the BBC decided to replace their London Radio Dance Band, which, for the past decade, had been a feature of Saturday-evening listening in homes across Britain, with the first BBC Dance Orchestra, led by Jack Payne. Within two years, his seven broadcasts per week, recording sessions, and personal appearances with the band had made him the most popular bandleader in Britain. At that time, broadcasts of records or a program of music for an evening's listening or dancing would contain a real mixture of styles. Jazz-orientated arrangements would be aired after popular ballads of the day, along with novelty or comedy numbers. Well known and loved was Jack Payne's rendering of "Muckin' About the Garden." Composed by "Q. Cumber" (generally thought to be Leslie Sarony, author of many humorous songs of the 1920s), this mildly risqué song ends as follows:

> If your rhubarb's far too forward
> Simply bend it back!

By the early 1930s, then, many British bands, both famous and less known, but practically all male, were playing arrangements in a mixture of styles, unlike many of their American counterparts.

But change was in the air.

2

CHANGING TIMES: THE 1930s

The Great Depression of the early 1930s affected the people of Britain and America in different ways. Though American musicians suffered because of the Depression, the New Deal programs of President Franklin D. Roosevelt (1882–1945) supported them as never before. Federal projects sponsored radio programs, commissioned new work from composers, and sought out American musicians to feature in recordings. In much smaller Britain, the financial squeeze was felt strongly by musicians but much more outside London than in the exclusive West End nightclubs where most of the best big bands played to moneyed audiences. This period showed the divisions in British society very clearly: the north-south divide and the gulf between the lives of those who had jobs or personal wealth and those who were unemployed.

Even throughout the economic doldrums, the London social scene was lively, the theaters, cinemas, and concert halls well attended. It was common for those who could afford it to go out to the cinema two or three times a week. In fact, although many people lost their jobs, those who kept them benefited from the Depression in a certain way, because prices fell and they could buy more. More money was available for holidays, cars, electrical goods, and entertainment. Hours of work and holiday entitlement were improved for workers who now had time and money to enjoy their leisure.

However, in the country as a whole, unemployment was high, rising to 2.5 million (25 percent of the workforce) in 1933. Worst hit were the centers of heavy industry in Northern Ireland, Scotland, Wales, and the north of England, already struggling because they had not modernized after World War I and had been badly affected by competition from other countries. Under the weight of the Depression, they finally crumbled. In Jarrow, a shipbuilding town in the northeast of England, after almost every man had lost his job, the townsfolk organized a march to London—a crusade to gather support and seek government assistance. The famous Jarrow March, 207 people strong, arrived at the Palace of Westminster on October 31, 1932. But there was no help forthcoming. They were told to go home and work out their own salvation—and given one pound each for the train journey back to Jarrow! Their shipyard never reopened.

Despite the many economic problems of the early 1930s—or perhaps because of them—dance music continued to be popular. Whether they lived in the north or south of the country, whether rich enough to enjoy dancing in exclusive hotels or just able to afford a wireless set at home, people could enjoy the exciting music of the big bands and dance to them. Every town and city wanted to hear the music, which allowed many big bands to tour the country. Families changed their meal times so that they could hear radio shows dedicated to broadcasting big band music. Record sales soared. Until about 1935, the bands tended to stick to the melody as it was written, and vocals would be sung sweetly (often in a tenor voice) and in tune with the melody. But bit by bit, American influence made itself felt, and in Britain the public took to bands with some pretensions to swing. Most popular were the sounds of Jack Hylton, Lew Stone, Roy Fox, and Bert Ambrose rather than the sweet bands. But whatever the music style, big bands provided the soundtrack to the 1920s and 1930s.

According to musicologist and music historian Sherrie Tucker, the beginning of the swing era is usually given as either 1932—the year Duke Ellington recorded and released "It Don't Mean a Thing (If It Ain't Got That Swing)"—or as August 1935. In the summer of

1935, Benny Goodman was touring his band, when in late August they arrived at the Palomar Ballroom in Los Angeles. The tour so far had not been a great success; in Denver a ballroom manager had insisted the band play waltzes when disgruntled patrons began demanding their money back. On the night of August 21, the set was in progress without much crowd reaction. In frustration, Benny started the band playing Fletcher Henderson's arrangement of "King Porter Stomp," with Gene Krupa providing the drumbeat. The kids screamed for more. NBC's microphones picked up the broadcast, and the rest of the tour was a howling success. The final booking for the band, a three-week engagement at the Congress Hotel in Chicago, turned into a stay of eight months, and according to many, "swing" had arrived.

However, this interpretation of the start of the phenomenon ignores the fact that black musicians, including Fletcher Henderson, Duke Ellington, and Count Basie, had been playing big band music characterized by a swing tempo at least ten years before it was purported to have begun with Goodman. Commenting on the "arrival" of swing to the jazz venues of Fifty-Second Street in Manhattan, Billie Holiday observed, "They could get away with calling it new because millions of squares hadn't taken a trip to 131st Street. If they had, they could have dug swing for twenty years."

And what was "swing"? Its exact definition is difficult to pin down. But perhaps it could be said to be music often arranged for a large dance band in a jazz style but marked by a smoother beat and more-flowing phrasing than Dixieland and having fewer complex harmonies and rhythms than modern jazz. Swing contains a strong rhythmic element that encourages dancers and listeners to move in time to the music. But perhaps the best definition is one given by jazz pianist Fats Waller. When asked once what swing is, he replied "Lady, if you gotta ask, you ain't got it!"

Unlike in Britain, 1930s America saw the emergence of many all-women bands, both white and black, and very much linked to the trend in band music toward swing. America's tradition of high school bands afforded musically inclined girls the opportunity to develop their skills as band instrumentalists. Helen Lewis and Her All-Girl Jazz Syncopators and Babe Egan and Her Hollywood Red Heads were early successes, and in 1927 the Parisian Red Heads, who hailed from Indiana, billed themselves as "The World's Greatest Girl Band." Obviously red hair was considered modern and appropriate to iconoclast women playing jazz.

By the mid 1930s, there were a few more significant all-female bands, most of which continued in their predecessors' lead, performing the vaudeville circuit; there were even some women playing alongside men in bands. Many of the bands with all-female players were led by men—for example, bandleader Phil Spitalny. But there were women bandleaders too, and successful enough to be heard on radio—like Lil-Hardin's All-Girl Band, for example, that performed regularly on the NBC Radio Network. Bands associated with historically black educational institutions performed dance music and blues vocals and were known for their ability to really swing—like the International Sweethearts of Rhythm, whose founding members were students at Piney Woods Country Life School, and the Prairie View Co-eds, from Prairie View A & M University.

Most of the few women's bands that have made it into histories of jazz and swing in the United States are white and considered "glamorous." Despite such bands as Ina Ray Hutton's Melodears, Dolly Dawn and Her Dawn Patrol, or Phil Spitalny's Hour of Charm Orchestra being serious professional jazz musicians, it was not primarily their *music* for which they were famed. A key element in their success was their ability to "reproduce images of idealized white womanhood." And the lineup of such bands included strings and harps, which supposedly emphasized femininity "to counterbalance the shocking (titillating?) appearance of women playing trombones, tubas, trumpets, and drums." Like their sister musicians across the Atlantic, the coming war would change their fortunes.

In Britain, women in bands seem to have been conspicuous by their absence, except as singers. This is not to say there were *no* women instrumentalists in popular music before the 1920s. By 1921, 76 percent of musicians and music teachers were female, but they could not belong, as the men could, to professional orchestras or indeed be part of professional church and university music. In response to this historical exclusion, from the turn of the twentieth century onward women had joined together to form ensembles of various sizes to play in theaters, restaurants, and large department stores. And of course, in the war years spanning 1914 to 1918, as too in the war a quarter century later, there was a hole to be filled in the entertainment industry as men went off to fight. Anyone reading British romances during the first quarter of the twentieth century will be familiar with the description of lovers meeting at the Lyons' Corner Houses to the tuneful background of ladies' orchestras.

But it was in the 1920s that women became more active in jazz and dance bands, playing instruments not previously thought appropriate. World War I had loosened the social and sexual controls on women, allowing them more freedom to associate informally with men. And after the horrors of the war, women were determined to live life to the full. Dancing to jazz bands afforded a new female expression, along with wearing short skirts, smoking cigarettes, and bobbing one's hair. Bubbling too since the 1800s was the battle for women's suffrage. It was a hard and sometimes tragic fight. By 1918, women over thirty were able to vote, but in 1928 British women were fully enfranchised, on the same terms as British men.

Even though many women musicians were far away from the fashionable London scene, they could all hear the bands on the radio and develop an ambition to play professionally. But pursuing such a career path wasn't easy. Unlike in the United States, Britain had no tradition of high school bands, and any opportunity to play in brass bands was mostly confined to women brought up in the north of England, where a rich tradition of community bands based around local industry had been in existence since the mid-1800s. However, British all-girl bands were extremely popular and successful between the wars. Some of these bands were led by men—Don Rico, Rudy Starita, and Teddy Joyce perhaps best known among them. But there were also women bandleaders. Edna Croudson's Rhythm Girls, an all-female sextet, was performing at least as early as 1928 and continued well into the 1930s. Well-known too in the United Kingdom at that time were Blanche Coleman and Her All-Girl Band, Gloria Faye's band of all-female musicians, and Dorothy Marno's all-women lineup.

Many such bands lasted only a few years, and others are entirely forgotten today. In 1927, Ynet Miles decisively won an open-band contest in London against all-male bands, although at the time disparaging comments were made by rivals about the advantages that pretty girls had over the male contestants. The implication was that looks rather than musical ability had swung the vote. Despite such success however, Ynet's band seems to have disappeared from the scene by the 1930s.

Almost all of the women bandleaders led all-female bands rather than male or mixed-gender bands, but there were a few exceptions in the United States. Lil Hardin Armstrong was a pianist, composer, arranger, and bandleader as well as Louis Armstrong's second wife. She helped her young husband, whom she had met in the 1920s as a fellow player in trumpeter King Oliver's small group, to step out on his own, and she taught him to read music. She also played a key role as pianist, musical director, and composer for Armstrong's Hot Five and Hot Seven studio ensembles. After her separation from Armstrong in 1931, she went on to lead several more bands, including two all-women groups, and made numerous recordings for the Decca label.

Blanche Calloway, older sister of singer and bandleader Cab Calloway, was a singer and bandleader in her own right. Reportedly she influenced her younger brother's style and stage presentation, and in 1921 she became the first woman to lead a big band, the otherwise-all-male Joy Boys. As a bandleader who was both black and female in the early twentieth century, Blanche battled both racism and sexism. That band broke up in 1938, and she formed an all-female band in 1940, which she ran until 1944.

But perhaps the most impressive music career of a woman in the 1930s, seemingly self-made without overreliance on personal male contacts, is that of pianist, composer, and arranger Mary Lou Williams. Born Mary Elfrieda Scruggs in Atlanta, Georgia, she started performing with saxophonist John Williams as a teenager, marrying him in 1927. A few years later, Williams followed her husband to Kansas City, where she began performing with the Clouds of Joy, a Kansas City band. In addition to providing the group's piano accompaniment throughout the 1930s, she also composed and arranged much of its music. Her success with the Clouds of Joy meant Williams was soon sending compositions and arrangements to bandleaders such as Tommy Dorsey, Earl Hines, Benny Goodman, and Duke Ellington. Williams remained an integral part of the swing scene throughout the 1930s.

However, despite such successes of certain women musicians, jazz critic George Simon echoed a popular belief of the time when he wrote that "Only God can make a tree, and only men can play good jazz." Joining the staff of American music magazine *Metronome* in 1935, Simon became editor-in-chief in 1939. Originally a dance band publication when he began working there, *Metronome* became the jazz magazine second in popularity only to *DownBeat*, and Simon was probably the most influential jazz commentator during the swing era. So, what he said was believed by his readers.

Although female singers were generally accepted and often spotlighted with big bands, female instrumentalists found the going tough. And even when they managed to find employment, reviewers usually commented on their looks, their clothing, and their effect on male audience members rather than their playing. Later in the late 1930s and early 1940s when the draft and call-up for World War II depleted the ranks of male musicians in America and Britain, more all-women bands and combos of various sizes were established. At first they were led by men, but soon women began taking up the baton. These bands provided opportunities for women to play instruments that they had not been typically encouraged to play—cornet, trumpet, sax, and drums. Many of these new professional women brass players migrated south from the north of England, where they had learned their instruments alongside fathers and brothers, playing in the community brass bands so popular there. And slowly too, over many years, opportunities for women to play alongside men in mixed line-ups increased.

But in 1935, when swing was hot and the big bands were everywhere—touring the United Kingdom, on the radio, and making records—band line-ups were essentially all male, and women instrumentalists still struggled to make an impact. Opportunities were limited by both overt and unintentional male chauvinism. In those days, war seemed distant—despite rumblings of approaching conflict—and bandleaders were still confident in their ability to recruit male players. While over time women instrumentalists were slowly becoming more accepted, many supported Simon's assertion, either actively or implicitly, that women could not play jazz. Achieving success as a woman band member, let alone a leader, proved to be a constant battle.

But things were about to change. A young woman saxophonist from Yorkshire arrived in London. She was confident, intelligent, and intent on long-term success.

Her name? Ivy Benson.

3

IVY

Holbeck, a suburb of Leeds in Yorkshire, England, was not the best place to be born. Nor was November 1913, with World War I on the horizon, the best time.

Holbeck, at one time a small hamlet on the fringes of Leeds, had been absorbed into the city by the mid-nineteenth century and had become a hub of engineering works and other heavy industry. Described at the start of that century as one of the most crowded, one of the most filthy, one of the most unpleasant, and one of the most un-healthy villages in the county of York, the slums had been cleared after cholera epidemics in 1832 and 1849. But by the time of Ivy's birth, the area had once again become poor with old, low standard housing.

Ivy Benson had, of course, no choice about when to be born. She arrived in the exceptionally mild winter weather of the year 1913, the third child of her parents in the space of only three years. She was born at her grandparents' public house, The Malt Shovel, in Lowerhead Road, Leeds, but her parents, Douglas Rolland Benson and Mary Jane Mead, soon took their new daughter back to their home in a small stone house nearby. Despite the presumed delight of having a new little girl, it must also have been a sad time for the family. The mild weather did not help her eldest brother Thomas's health, and he died of diphtheria in 1914, leaving her parents with another small boy, then just one year old, and baby Ivy. When Ivy was six, the family moved to

59 Cemetery Road, Beeston, and Ivy went to the local school, Saint Luke's in Beeston Hill, Leeds.

The family was poor, largely due to her father being a heavy drinker and earning little. Ivy reported that much of the furniture in the house in those early years was composed of wooden boxes and that her mother scrubbed steps to supplement the family's income. However, her father, although a riveter by trade, was also a very competent musician. He played lead trombone with the Leeds Symphony Orchestra and also at the Leeds Empire Theatre on Briggate. He played cello too. Although rarely playing outside an orchestra, he did take to the stage once as one of the Ten Loonies, a troupe of musical characters. Despite the Bensons' lack of money, the family must have had a piano in the house, or at least ready access to one—perhaps at her grandparent's pub—as Ivy took piano lessons from the age of five. Her father was ambitious for his only daughter and would threaten to smack her if she didn't practice.

But he needn't have worried; she loved it. She was a born performer, and her talent for music was quickly recognized. In 1923 at only nine years old, she made her first broadcast on the BBC's *Children's Hour* playing "In a Persian Market," and just over a year later she sang "Yes, We Have No Bananas" at a children's talent contest. Florrie Forde, who presented the prize to Ivy, was one of the most popular stars of the early twentieth-century music hall, specializing in songs in which the audience were invited to join. Presumably the entertainer was on tour and playing in Leeds that week. Young Ivy would have been excited to meet her. At this time, too, Ivy helped support her family by playing the piano at working men's clubs around Leeds, accompanying a friend of her father who played the banjo. Billed as Baby Benson, Ivy was paid five shillings for each gig, just over thirteen pounds today—a useful addition to the family's income.

Despite her father's dream that his daughter would become a professional classical pianist, Ivy had other ideas. She was fond of German music and particularly enthusiastic about American jazz. One day, Ivy heard Benny Goodman on the radio playing the saxophone and said to herself, "That's me!" She decided that she wanted to be a professional band musician. But the prospect of such a life after her school days was most unlikely in the Leeds of 1928; such opportunities were remote dreams. However, there did seem to be a chance that her future might be different from that of most girls she knew when she won a scholarship to Leeds School of Art. She was a talented young artist, and she started with high hopes. But it was not to last. There was not enough money for the family to support her studies. Equipment and books were too expensive, and regretfully, she left her education. There being no alternative, Ivy started work, first in a shoe department of a large store, and then, like the majority of her contemporaries, she joined the workforce of Montague Burton, a major gentlemen's clothes manufacturer in the city.

Sir Montague Maurice Burton, born Meshe Osinsky, was a Lithuanian refugee who opened his first business, a draper's shop, in Chesterfield, Derbyshire, in 1904. In 1921 Burton began to develop the Hudson Road factory in the Burmantofts district of Leeds, which gradually became the biggest clothing factory in the world. It employed ten thousand on the site and produced over thirty thousand suits a week and was the biggest employer in the city, the heart of the Montague Burton business empire. Of Burton's fourteen factories, the one in the Burmantofts district of Leeds was designated the flagship, and by the 1930s he also owned a chain of five hundred menswear shops. They were the most distinctive shops on British high streets, with bold art deco motifs, including stylized stonework elephant heads, faience panels, bronzed metal, and polished granite. Many of these shop fronts still exist on Britain's high streets, although they are no longer owned by Burton's.

"Good clothes develop a man's self-respect," Burton believed. He was dedicated to providing high-quality made-to-measure suits at a reasonable price, offering "a five-guinea suit for fifty-five shillings." Men would start work at fourteen as barrow boys and if thought good enough would be apprenticed as tailors and cutters. But the men were far outnumbered by women. The Burton factories were filled with vast workrooms of machinists, with parents and children often working on the same production line. The Burton factory in Burmantofts was described by former tailor Sam Bernstein as "a town itself."

Burton was an unusually foresighted employer, supporting his workforce in ways that were many years ahead of their time. He provided a works canteen, which meant that whole families could feed themselves cheaply and well, and workers were offered a generous health and retirement pension. Montague Burton chose to center his empire in Leeds because it was the center of Britain's textile industry, providing ample access to skilled tailors and machinists. Although the presence of a large employer in the area was positive in many ways, especially for women, the demand for skilled tailors and the availability of cheaper suits meant that many small tailoring shops, unable to compete with the low prices at Burton's, were forced to shutter, their tailors obliged to work in the new factory.

Burton's in Leeds no longer exists, but the words "Monty" (for Montague) and "Burton" have entered the English language. After World War II, Burton became a major supplier of suits to demobilized forces, issuing each serviceman a full outfit. They were given the choice of a blue or brown "de-mob" suit, plus shoes, a shirt, and a tie. These were not made to measure, so the fit was somewhat hit-or-miss. However, if the soldier, airman, or sailor happened to be one of a few standard fittings, he would look very smart in the suit. The phrase "the full monty" may find its origins in these outfits. It is most likely that the phrase "gone for a Burton"—the euphemism for a pilot's being shot down and killed in wartime—is more likely to refer to Burton Ales, although there are some who think that it might refer to being dismissed, demobbed, or rejected from the services and therefore changing a military uniform for a Burton's suit.

In 1928 the huge Burton's factory claimed the fourteen-year-old Ivy as one of its young clerks. She earned eighteen shillings a week, very reasonable pay for her age. It wasn't a bad place to work, and she was one of many girls and women who worked together. Most of her workmates would have been perfectly content to work in the factory

until they married and then return after child-rearing, staying until retirement. But Ivy had other ideas. She still wanted to make her career
as a professional musician—a saxophonist. She bought her own alto
saxophone from Kitchen's Music Shop in the center of Leeds, paying
it off on hire purchase. She would give her mother her wages, except
for a small amount of spending money, but even so, she managed to
find two shillings and sixpence a week for the payments.

She learned the saxophone easily in two months. Her father played
a number of instruments and taught her to play the clarinet too, which
she took a little longer to master. Influenced by listening to famous
jazz clarinetist Artie Shaw, she developed a love for that instrument
too, and even though she was still very young, her father arranged for
her to practice with the grown men at the famous local pub, Lupton
Whitelocks. She would sit at the end of a row of eight clarinetists,
where she would play the easy parts.

Every workday saw Ivy at the factory from 8 a.m. until 6 p.m.,
when she would head off for the evening to play clarinet and saxophone at dances to supplement the family income. Pay was seven
shillings and sixpence a gig, good money in the mid 1920s, more than
a third of her weekly wage at the factory. She could play jazz as well
as the sweeter band music, and her precocious talent was in demand
locally. But despite her amateur success, she longed for the opportunity to leave her life in the factory for good and become a career
musician. Although throughout her life she was to give the outward
impression that she could cope with the lifestyle of a peripatetic musician, at this early stage in her career, she revealed to an interviewer
much later in life, she suffered a nervous breakdown. Working in the
factory and then playing until two or three in the morning was taking
its toll; she could not do both jobs. She left the factory and concen-
trated on her music.

Her big chance came sooner than she could have expected. In
1929 the organist at the Paramount Cinema in Leeds contacted her
father with a request. Henry Croudson was well known in musical
circles in the city, and when the magnificent new theater opened

several years later in 1932, he would secure the coveted job of playing the mighty Wurlitzer organ that rose from the depths of the movie hall each evening to accompany silent films. Back in 1928, his wife, Edna, had formed an all-girls sextet, Edna Croudson's Rhythm Girls, and they were booked for the summer season of 1929 in Bridlington, a resort town on the Yorkshire coast. Edna had, unexpectedly, just lost her saxophonist and desperately needed a replacement. Henry knew that Digger Benson had a talented daughter and encouraged her to contact his wife. Ivy immediately wrote to Edna, and the direct approach worked. After a short audition in a seaside café in Bridlington, Ivy got the job. Still only fifteen, she was now a professional musician.

While playing at the seaside, she met Reg Connelly, a successful songwriter and music publisher along with his partner, Jimmy Campbell. This meeting marked the start of both a personal and professional association that would span more than twenty years. Reg immediately recognized Ivy's talent and was keen for her to move to London. However, she was still very young, so she toured with Edna Croudson for a few more years, until 1935.

Ivy's only remaining sibling, a brother, had died tragically at the age of eighteen, and she must have felt some responsibility toward her grieving mother and father. Even so, she made the hard choice to follow her dreams, moving south, to London. She would remain very close to her parents, especially her father, throughout her life, and they would later live with her for many years.

Arriving in London to further her career, Ivy played alto sax and clarinet in a rather sleazy club opposite the Windmill Theatre as a member of a three-piece band and hoped for better things. Always broke in these early days, she used to burn the end of soggy clarinet reeds to dry and sharpen them up for reuse. She couldn't afford to keep buying new ones. Often overlooked by her biographers is the fact that she became a bandleader before the war. Appalled at the lack of jobs and poor pay for women musicians, she decided to do something about it. She formed an all-girl band of five instrumentalists—all much older than she and, as she remembered, "dreadful musicians"—with whom she toured dance halls.

How Ivy met Teddy Joyce, the Canadian bandleader and crooner, is not absolutely clear, but most sources believe that he heard her play saxophone at the club and was impressed. Teddy Joyce was a showman, and after arriving in Britain in January 1934 had enjoyed a meteoric rise on the British dance band scene. He was brimming with personality, a very good dancer, and a violinist of a sort. Because of his showmanship, "he could make ordinary fiddle playing sound like a masterpiece of melody," and the bands he fronted were the background for his extrovert activities on the cabaret floor. In his first year in Britain he played at the Kit Kat Club in the Haymarket, toured for Paramount, and was engaged at the Dorchester Hotel and the London Palladium, all with great success.

His orchestra played for the opening of Paramount Pictures' new theater in Liverpool on October 1 that year and for the 1935 New Year celebrations at their theater in Glasgow. His Teddy Joyce Orchestra even appeared in the movie *Radio Parade of 1935* alongside comedian Will Hay and a wealth of variety talent. Some ups and downs in his career followed, including running his own nightclub, the Continental, in the West End and touring a repertory company with his new wife, Chili Bouchier. Unfortunately, both the club and the company, while initially successful, fell apart due to financial problems, and he was forced to disband his orchestra in 1939.

But true to his ebullient form, Joyce bounced back a few weeks later, forming an all-girl orchestra. The band was an all-female lineup of musicians with him as the bandleader, and he had obtained a contract to tour a show called *Radio Rodeo*. Teddy asked Ivy to play lead sax for Teddy Joyce and the Girlfriends. Although the pay was a paltry three pounds a week, she jumped at the chance. It was during this tour that she met Jack Hylton, who would become a close friend and adviser. Later the famous bandleader would open doors for her when many other male bandleaders were making it difficult for more women to enter the profession.

Teddy Joyce's success, however, was not to last. By late 1939, his career had become erratic. He had formed a seven-piece group to play at the newly opened version of the old Kit Kat Club in Regent Street, and he combined this with afternoon and evening stage appearances. Exhausted from his work and constant clowning, he collapsed on stage late that year, and by early 1940 he would be dead at the young age of thirty-six. It was becoming obvious to Ivy that working in an all-girl orchestra for Teddy Joyce was not going to be a steady job, and so in 1939, encouraged by some of her bandmates, she decided that it was the ideal time to form her own band. Twelve of the Teddy Joyce "girl-friends," dissatisfied with their lot and probably realizing their future would be more secure with Ivy, joined her.

4

EARLY WAR

War was declared on September 3, 1939. The almost immediate in-troduction of the blackout and more importantly the start of the Blitz in London in 1940 caused massive disruption to the entertainment industry. The first reaction of the authorities in Britain was to close down nightclubs and all places of entertainment for fear of air raids. There was instant opposition, the outraged playwright George Bernard Shaw writing to the newspapers, "May I be allowed to protest vehe-mently against the order to close all theatres and picture houses during the war. It seems to me a masterstroke of unimagined stupidity. . . . What agent of Chancellor Hitler is it who suggested that we should all cower in darkness and terror for the duration?"

Whether the playwright's intervention was a factor or not, re-strictions were eased very quickly, and London theaters reopened, among them the Windmill, which offered a program of humor, music, dancing girls, and nude tableaux vivants. Most provincial theaters such as the Blackpool Grand Theatre stayed open. These theaters prospered like never before and were busy all fifty-two weeks of the year. Blackpool was a major war center, and the Grand catered to the holidaymakers who continued to come as a morale booster, but also to four thousand relocated civil servants, thirty-eight thousand evacuees, forty-five thousand British service personnel billeted in the town, and later the eleven thousand Americans stationed at Warton, twelve miles away. The Victoria Theatre in Burnley, in the industrial northwest of England, became the unlikely home for the bombed-out Old Vic and Sadler's Wells companies, and in 1941 Sybil Thorndike appeared in a season of Shakespeare there. The company went on a tour of the North of England and South Wales, playing schools, miners' institutes, and village halls. A production of *Macbeth* in South Wales was very well received, and the great actress wrote at the time, "This is the theatre that we liked best—getting right in amongst people. Afterwards they all come round and talk to us."

For those employed in the music business, the first effects of war were dislocation and unemployment; musicians were caught up in the turmoil abroad and panic at home. But gradually, as the war tightened its grip, it was realized that more and not less entertainment was needed to support the war effort. People needed to keep up their spirits for the possibly long, difficult period ahead. Soon people were back again dancing. Thanks to Jack Hylton, Ivy's new band was lucky enough to gain a booking at the Ritz in Manchester. Her real career as a bandleader had begun. Before Ivy, very few bands had women playing trombones and trumpets, and so audiences came at first to see Ivy and her ensemble out of curiosity. All the band members, including Ivy, were paid nine guineas a week. It was tough for her financially, as the bandleader was expected to provide dresses, music stands, and the other incidentals of performance. She wasn't going to be rich any time soon, but she was doing what she wanted—leading a band.

Then, once again with the assistance of Jack Hylton, she secured a booking at Covent Garden. The opera house had closed at the start of the war, but within a few months of the closure, the popular ballroom chain Mecca bought a five-year lease on the building. They raised the floor of the stalls to the level of the stage, installed parquet flooring, and created a bandstand behind the proscenium arch. On December 23, 1939, the Royal Opera House reopened its doors as a dance hall. For the duration of the war, Covent Garden became one of London's most-enduring entertainment hotspots. Dancing was an essential diversion for servicemen and women on leave, as well as for Londoners;

dances ran virtually every afternoon and evening during the war, with evening-only openings on Saturdays. Entrance was limited to 1,500 dancers, but it wasn't unusual for numbers to exceed this by several hundred.

Organizations such as Mecca offered the best openings for anyone attempting to break into the world of professional musicianship, and Ivy was lucky. Her band was one of only five that rotated to provide dance music. The Ivy Benson Rhythm Girls, a show band of fifteen female musicians directed by Ivy, was described by *London Ballroom News* as having "solidity and vigour." Audiences were surprised by the high standard of their playing. They weren't just a novelty act; the band could compete with the men.

But there were key inequalities. It was still a man's world. The Musicians' Union was still resentful of women players. Ivy's "girls" were paid less than the men. And unlike her male counterparts, Mecca would not buy her as a whole band. As bandleader she was paid six pounds, ten shillings a week, and her players five guineas each. Ivy was under no illusions about the job she had to do. She knew that if her band was to succeed, her musicians had to be as good as the men. She admitted that at the time most male players were better than women— not surprising, perhaps, seeing as women had so few opportunities to develop their professional skills. Some of the girls thought that they could get by with "a few tootles and good looks," Ivy recounted, but she was having none of that. She was a tough taskmaster. If her girls' band was to earn the same money and play in the same places as men, they had to play as well as them.

As the war progressed and many male players joined the forces, bands were decimated, and suddenly there were unimagined opportunities for women instrumentalists. However, it was not an easy job to recruit female musicians at that time; Ivy wasn't the only bandleader looking for the best instrumentalists and singers. There were no queues of unemployed women professionals waiting to be hired. Ivy had to start from scratch by recruiting likely candidates with little experience and then coaching them. But she seemed always to have a keen eye for spotting musical ability whether developed or not, and she made sure that she secured those young women with the most potential for her band.

The decision to form an all-girl band was timely. Many of the instrumentalists in the existing big bands were being called up to the armed services, and at the same time there was a surge in the interest in dance music to entertain civilians and service personnel on leave. As early as 1941 the BBC broadcast dance music as an important morale booster, and there was a new need that developed: entertainment needed to be taken to wherever the troops were stationed. Despite the recognition that such music on the radio was important, the government resisted classifying dance musicians as an essential occupation, and critics thought them unmanly shirkers. As the call-up decimated the ranks of instrumentalists, the quality of dance music declined.

To counteract this, the BBC developed the Dance Band Scheme, which gave indefinite contracts to Jack Payne, who played the unadventurous middle-brow music that the BBC favored, and to Geraldo, whose tastes and playlists were more up-to-date. Victor Silvester, however, was the bandleader who most managed to reconcile dance music with wartime manliness, positioning dancing as an activity that supported wartime goals of fitness and social harmony. He had seen active service as a young boy in World War I when he lied about his age and had won the Italian Bronze Medal of Military Valour. He was part of over 6,500 broadcasts, and his popular BBC Dancing Club series started in 1941. From 1943 to 1944, influenced by the influx of American servicemen into the United Kingdom, Silvester directed a series of recordings made especially for jive dancing. No one could doubt his bravery. Whether broadcasting entertaining music for listeners or dancers, male dance musicians had to position themselves carefully as fully masculine.

At least that wasn't a problem for Ivy's band, which was obviously all female. But it wasn't easy for them to gain public acceptance. Though initially curiosity brought spectators to their shows, eventually they began coming for the music, and slowly things got better for Ivy and her band. She was insistent that her women players were the best she could get. She wanted them to look attractive on stage but above all to be excellent instrumentalists. Many promising young women were invited to audition and, if good, might even find themselves playing that very night. Initially her band included the twelve instrumentalists who had left Teddy Joyce's band with her, but over the many years that followed, she needed a plentiful supply of talent, constantly having to replace band members who left. Their youth, vitality, and glamor were magnets to the men who came to hear them play. Both during the war and for many years afterward, British servicemen and GIs as well as civilians attracted the girls into marriage. Ivy told one story of playing in Stuttgart when a girl, Marjorie from Manchester, asked if she could go and see her American suitor, whom she'd spotted in the audience. "Oh, there's Skip. Can I go and talk to him?" the girl had asked. "Yes, Marjorie," Ivy had replied; "don't be long." Marjorie jumped off the bandstand, and Ivy never saw her again. She had to take over the piano for the rest of the month.

In 1940 Ivy and her Rhythm Girls appeared in an all-girl revue called Meet the Girls, starring comedian Hylda Baker. It was billed as a female attack on the blackout blues. After the revue ended in the summer of 1940, Ivy signed with the Mecca organization and so began a number of years touring venues in Britain, mostly under the auspices of Entertainments National Service Association—ENSA, as they were known—entertaining both civilians and troops. From 1940 until the end of the war, Ivy fronted a number of variously sized bands, from twelve to twenty-three players, sometimes with a string section, sometimes without.

Being in big cities at this time was dangerous. That autumn, the Germans initiated what would be an eight-month bombing offensive, flattening large swaths of cities across the United Kingdom. On September 7, 1940, the Blitz started, and London was systematically bombed by the Luftwaffe for fifty-six out of the following fifty-seven days and nights. The girls in the band had their gas masks with them on stage, and upon arriving at new venues Ivy made sure that they all knew the way to the shelters and to their digs. The band was in

Manchester when that city was bombed in 1941, and Ivy remembered running hard, hand-in-hand with one of her youngest girls to get back to their digs, with the sirens screaming and air raid wardens urging them to get down into the shelters. But Ivy wouldn't go into the shelters; she preferred to see out the raids in the digs. If she was going to die, she said, she would rather it not be with tons of concrete on her head. If the band was in the middle of a performance when the sirens sounded, she would gather up her brood and shepherd them to safety.

The bombs seemed to be following them about, as shortly after Manchester they faced another spate of heavy bombing in Glasgow. In London, too, playing at Covent Garden, there was always the risk of sudden death. In 1941, at the height of World War II, the West Indian Orchestra, led by the twenty-seven-year-old Ken "Snakehips" Johnson, was resident at The Café de Paris in London's West End, on Coventry Street. It was a very small club; the dance floor could only hold a few couples at a time. The club was down a long, steep staircase, far down under street level, and because of this, the patrons felt quite safe. Unfortunately, on March 8, during a German air raid on London, one of the bombs unerringly found the club's airshaft. Over thirty people were killed outright, including Ken Johnson and his tenor sax. Over sixty more were seriously injured. Even worse but perhaps less well-known was the 1943 raid on London that killed seventy-three people, including soldiers and airmen, who had been dancing at the Palace Dance Hall in Putney as well as many in the milk bar underneath. Hundreds more were injured. Sadly, by this time both the public and performers had become used to bombings and were sometimes blasé about the dangers. And although the air raid warning had sounded, the band had continued to play on and the dancers to dance—until disaster struck.

There must always have been the fear at the back of people's minds that the bombs could bring death. But Ivy remembered the time as mostly a happy one, the servicemen cheerful and full of fun despite the thought that they might be shipped out on the morrow to an unknown future. She said that she never worried about the bombing in the earlier part of the war; her attitude was that if something were to happen, it would happen. But something changed for Ivy in the later years, especially in 1944 when the V-1 bombings started. These early cruise missiles, colloquially known as "doodlebugs," screamed upon launch and were very frightening. In October 1944, the last V-1 site in range of Britain was silenced, and the raids began focusing on Antwerp and other Belgian targets. But the previous month the Germans had begun a new offensive on London with V-2 rockets—considerably larger than doodlebugs and potentially even more dangerous. However, the V-2 was not considered as scary as the doodlebug, since, being so fast, it was never seen or heard—until it landed with a loud *whoomph* noise. Casualties had little time to be afraid. Despite all the dangers, Ivy and the girls became used to working in London and other enemy-targeted cities.

Touring the band in wartime led to other problems—shaky finances. Ivy had negotiated a deal that would give her and the band 60 percent of the takings, with the rest being retained by the booking agent. It seemed a good deal. But early bombings led to widespread fear, and the band sometimes played to more or less empty theaters. Sixty percent hardly paid for one trombone player, Ivy recalled later, and finding the money to pay her players was a constant headache. But as German air attacks became regular events in big cities, people grew more stoic and once again began flocking to dance halls.

By 1942 Ivy's band, which varied in size over the years, had grown to sixteen players and played in variety shows booked by Jack Hylton Management. Ivy secured a year's contract. The band was in great demand, working fifty-two weeks a year and struggling to take time off for breaks. Soon Ivy was top of the bill at venues like the Palace Theatre Manchester as well as Covent Garden and the London Palladium. To maintain this busy schedule, Ivy needed to keep her players and not lose them. Told by Jack Hylton that entertaining the troops for six weeks in a year would count as the equivalent of war work and that if she did this her players would not be conscripted, Ivy established links with the services early on.

As of the spring of 1941, every woman in Britain between the ages of eighteen and sixty was required to register and declare their family occupation. Upon interview, each selected from among a range of jobs that supported the war effort—though no women were required to bear arms. The National Service Act (No. 2) of December of that year legalized compulsory induction of women, at first only calling up single women between twenty and thirty years of age to serve. But by the following summer, almost 90 percent of all single women and 80 percent of married women were performing essential war work. As young unmarried women, all of Ivy's band members, and Ivy herself, were expected to contribute to the war effort. Sometimes Ivy had to go to the Ministry of Labour and plead for exemptions for those of her players who had been sent notices to report for war work. She was mostly successful, but at least one of her girls was sent to work on a capstan lathe in a factory.

Despite these travails, Ivy managed to secure enough instrumentalists for the band to tour military bases in Britain and also broadcast to troops, often under the auspices of ENSA. With her group of mostly very young women, braving bombs, wartime deprivations, and the determination of young men to steal her "girls," she set out resolutely to make a name for herself.

5

THE ENTERTAINMENTS NATIONAL SERVICE ASSOCIATION

In 1939, in an effort to provide entertainment for British armed forces personnel during World War II, entertainers Basil Dean and Leslie Hanson created the Entertainments National Service Association as a part of the Navy, Army, and Air Force Institutes (NAAFI). If occasionally the ENSA performances were more patriotic than skillful—sardonically nicknamed by troops as *Every Night Something Awful*, or Tommy Trinder's alternative, *Even NAAFI Stands Aghast*—thousands of performers of varying ability, from stars of stage and screen to the downright amateur, worked hard to keep the troops and workers entertained during the war. If the result of an off-key singer or amateur band was amusement at the expense of the performers, such events nevertheless relieved the monotony of life on military bases and in factories and were much anticipated.

ENSA's variety shows quickly expanded beyond the original purview to include performances in factories, mines, hospitals, and hostels and to organize radio broadcasts and performances in civilian concert halls and theaters. It grew and grew until almost all non-combatant members of the theatrical, variety, and musical professions were involved in one way or another. Manufacturers of theater and cinema equipment, scenery and lighting contractors, and costume and property makers all found their products in high demand. They had to ensure they were able to meet the requisition demands of ENSA's administrator, the Department of National Service Entertainment.

When the war started, Basil Dean was already immersed in the business of entertainment. He had founded Associated Talking Pictures, a British production and distribution company in 1929, and he was writer, director, and producer for many of the hit films of the 1930s, such as *The Show Goes On* with Gracie Fields and *Lorna Doone* with Margaret Lockwood. Dean was well placed to contact and involve many of the day's leading actors in his new venture and persuade them to join. He also built and ran Ealing Studios from 1930 until 1938, when he left the film industry.

Dean was not an easy man to work for or with; he was abrasive and got many people's backs up. But ENSA would never have existed without him. His was a civilian organization operating under military rules and regulations, and Dean fought like a tiger for his fledgling organization with a hostile press, the top brass in the military, civil servants, and above all the BBC, who made life difficult for him personally and for ENSA. But despite all the trials and tribulations of running such a vast undertaking, Dean was able to ensure that over 80 percent of all of Britain's entertainment industry provided service to ENSA and that by the time the war had ended over 2.6 million performances had been given to the services and workers in the United Kingdom, Northwest Europe, and other overseas commands. Despite criticisms of quality and jeers at the standard of some performers, "for every third-rate, end-of-the-pier act there was a George Formby or Gracie Fields."

The ENSA tried to be all things to all people, producing everything from Stars in Battledress, the RAF Gang Show, and variety concerts to Shakespeare, new plays, and ballet. In 1940, Sadler's Wells ballet company toured neutral Holland, where they performed *Les Patineurs* and *Dante Sonata* to critical acclaim. The dancers recalled seeing flowers thrown onto the stage for the first time—and this being Holland, they were spring flowers of tulips and daffodils. On

May 10, the Germans invaded Holland, and the company, with many very young dancers, fled the country with almost nothing. Costumes, scenery, stage equipment, and scores were left behind.

Despite performances by Ninette de Valois' critically acclaimed ballet company and participation by such legendary actors such as Laurence Olivier and Ralph Richardson, class conflict reared its head at ENSA performances. While regular troops wanted to see attractive girls, dancers, and comedy, military officers sent disapproving memos complaining of blue jokes and scantily clad women. In 1940 the Council for the Encouragement of Music and the Arts was established to help support and preserve British culture. The CEMA's mission, different from ENSA's, was directed at the home front rather than soldiers, airmen, and sailors. They also paid a higher wage rate and offered better traveling conditions and accommodation. Soon after its foundation, CEMA became associated with many stars and leading ensembles. Sadler's Wells ballet company, Ballet Rambert, and Ballet Jooss, for example, toured factories, garrisons, and hostels; and the Old Vic company toured Shakespeare through Welsh mining villages for several seasons. Rather than being seen as the preserve of well-to-do audiences in London as it had previously, ballet played to capacity houses during the war and found new fans. Opera, too, achieved new popularity as Sadler's Wells toured the industrial towns of the North. In 1945, CEMA became the Arts Council of Great Britain.

But ENSA was the means by which most workers and military personnel were entertained, and the roll call of ENSA performers is long. Well-known artists gave their time for the cause and took the comparatively derisive salary of ten pounds per week for all or donated it to good causes. In 1939, music hall great Gracie Fields performed for ENSA, even as she was recuperating from a breakdown and an operation to treat cervical cancer. Her show, headed by her old film producer Basil Dean, traveled to France to entertain the troops amid air raids, performing on the backs of open lorries and in war-torn areas. Fields was the first major artist to play behind enemy lines in Berlin. Though in 1939, just before war had been declared, Italy had signed the Pact of Steel, a military alliance with Germany, it was not until June 10, 1940, that Benito Mussolini declared war on both Great Britain and France. This changed the situation for Gracie, who had recently married an Italian. With Italy now an enemy to Britain, Gracie excused herself from future ENSA performances, leaving for North America, where she instead actively raised funds for wartime charities. Throughout the war, she occasionally returned to Britain, performing in factories and army camps around the country.

Some veteran performers such as Scottish comedian and singer Sir Harry Lauder came out of retirement to entertain the troops. And Florrie Forde—who in Leeds many years before had presented the young Ivy Benson with the dollhouse prize for winning a talent contest—also worked hard to support the war effort. Unfortunately, her time with ENSA was short, as she collapsed and died after singing for the troops in Aberdeen in April 1940. Other established performers from different parts of the industry included actress Peggy Ashcroft and comedian Arthur Askey. Tommy Handley, too, brought his talents to ENSA, his hit radio show, *It's That Man Again*, having kept Britain in stitches with its many catch phrases—"Can I do you now, sir?" and "It's being so cheerful as keeps me going"—and digs at Hitler. And not forgetting of course the young Vera Lynn, "the Forces' Sweetheart," who toured Egypt, India, and Burma as part of ENSA, giving outdoor concerts for the troops. She is remembered for nostalgic songs that reminded the servicemen of home, such as "We'll Meet Again" and "The White Cliffs of Dover."

But while it might be true that for every third-rate, end-of-the-pier performer there was a Gracie Fields, it is also true that for every Gracie Fields there were many less-polished artistes, dancers, musicians, comedians, and singers. To recruit entertainers, ENSA advertised in *The Stage* and other trade publications, and word spread quickly. Anyone who could "do a turn" was considered. The organization was inundated with applications, mostly from those who had been hardest hit by war: The pubs, clubs, and seaside venues where the performers previously would have been welcomed were no longer hiring. Many applications too came from those who saw ENSA as a chance to restart their failing careers or from those in amateur dramatic companies, anxious to offer their services and perhaps hoping to be discovered.

As well as gifted singers and musicians, ENSA featured saw players, contortionists, conjurors, clowns, and novelty acts. Revue star Joyce Grenfell was initially critical of the quality of some ENSA offerings. In 1943 she was asked to be the compere for a concert party performing shows in hospitals. She had her own spot for monologues but "had to endure being on the bill with enthusiastic but less-talented amateurs. . . . We had a husband and wife act with an accordion-concertina act which ended with him playing 'The Bluebells of Scotland' on two concertinas at the same time, one in each hand pressed against his chest and cymbals tied to his knees," she remembered. "His wife rang hand bells. Our singer, a statuesque blonde like a Staffordshire china Ceres, Goddess of Plenty . . . had a swooping soprano that plummily sang a trifle under the high notes."

But despite all the setbacks and criticisms, Basil Dean's motley crew risked life and limb touring Britain and later the Continent to perform, taking entertainment to those who badly needed it.

Getting around during the war was difficult. The performers were often performing in different places each day, from the Orkneys and Shetland in the north of Scotland to Plymouth on England's south-western coast, traveling by coach or train. The trains were crowded and uncomfortable, and often performers had to catch what sleep they could on the dirty floor of the swaying car. An added problem was that stations had no name boards during the war, making it quite difficult to know where exactly you were or whether you'd missed your stop. Coach travel too was tiring, although at least there might be space to hang costumes. It wasn't unusual for coaches to lose their way in the blackout, as road signs had also been removed. One performer reported how her party found themselves lost in the middle of the night on the Yorkshire Moors. It could be even worse in other theaters of war: ENSA parties traveling in Italy shortly after the country's surrender in September 1943 found themselves in danger from continuing fighting with the Germans. Sandy Powell—the well-known radio comedian known for his catchphrase, "Can you hear me, mother?"—reported that he played at a theater on the Adriatic one evening only to see it reduced to rubble on the following day.

The ENSA parties traveled throughout the year, often in cold and wet winter weather. There is a photograph of Tommy Handley and the cast of *ITMA* entertaining service personnel at Scapa Flow in the north of Scotland, Britain's main naval base during World War II. It shows them huddled up, bundled in fur coats, scarves, and boots against the biting cold of the Orkney weather, one woman even wearing a fur muff to keep her hands warm. It was even more difficult to adjust to different weather conditions as artists moved between the different countries where troops were based. The winter of 1943 was very cold in Italy, and some ENSA artists who had traveled there from North Africa in lightweight uniforms were caught unaware. Basil Dean said that it was so cold in Foggia, in the southeast of Italy, that an open brazier, visible through the flimsy backdrop, had to be kept burning throughout the show. That same winter in Italy, one ENSA company called Lucky Dip was moving on from playing in a hotel in Campobasso, near Monte Cassino. It was freezing cold, and blizzarding conditions prevented the drivers from seeing their route. They tried to turn around but became stuck in snowdrifts. The company was trapped for three days, during which the performers and their drivers drank melted snow and lived on meager rations. Eventually skiers brought more food, and finally a bulldozer arrived to rescue them. Joy Denny, one of the same concert party, remarked that when traveling behind battle lines they often saw hurriedly dug graves at the side of the road with simple crosses and the dead soldier's helmet. "Looking back, it was incredibly sad. . . . tragic, of course. . . . but at the time, you had to train yourself not to think about it too much. . . . We didn't really think about being killed, we were too busy traveling, rehearsing, and doing our shows."

There are many more stories of the difficulties and privations of wartime travel for the ENSA performers. But it is surely a testament to the organizational skills of ENSA travel planners that most of the performers reached their destinations, sometimes in heavily defended warzones, and that during the whole of the war there was only one ENSA casualty. Dancer Vivian Hole—whose stage name was Vivienne Fayre—was killed in the Netherlands in 1945 when a scenery truck in which she was a passenger ran over a landmine.

Life was not glamorous. Traveling around Britain, particularly when playing in factories, ENSA performers were lodged by the area manager in the cheapest lodgings. Sometimes these had to be changed at the last moment if planned houses had been bombed. One singer, who was still a teenager when recruited by ENSA, found herself sharing lodgings with the local prostitutes "whose language and behaviour were way outside anything she had experienced before." Getting an egg to eat was an occasion, and keeping stage costumes decent often required plugging in an iron to the light socket. Accommodation on military bases was not much better; they were often in Nissen huts, where buckets of water sufficed for both lavatory and washing facilities. Occasionally the party was lucky enough to perform at a requisitioned stately home where accommodation was infinitely better than usual.

The shows themselves were not easy to stage. In factories, which often had been changed from their peacetime use, facilities for performers were minimal. There was usually a tiny stage erected in the canteen where workers, who had little time to spare from their work, passed to and fro with their dinners while the performers worked hard to be heard above the chatter in the room. The performers then had to wait around to repeat their show for the night shift. It was a little better on military bases, where the stage might consist of a few tables pushed together in the hangar, canteen, or wherever the show was to be held, with old sacking for curtains. These slightly larger venues could cater to dancers who had a "tap mat," which was in sections so that it could be rolled up to be packed. There was little privacy. Changing stage costumes behind old curtains often risked offering the troops the gratifying sight of a shapely bare bottom through unnoticed holes. Even reaching the stage was not without problems. Fully dressed for the show, the performers had to find their way over duckboards and across muddy paths, carrying their stage shoes to protect them from the dirt.

Things could and did go wrong. Often! Apart from the chances of a show being cut short by strafing from enemy aircraft or the artists having to make a run for it when German troops attacked the bases where they were playing, there were other accidents and dramas. One girl, as a finale to her acrobatic act, released two doves, intended to alight prettily on her shoulder. But long hours of traveling had badly affected the doves. When released, one flew out and promptly fell to the ground, dead, amid screams from the performer. A comedian in another troupe wore long-toed boots and, as part of his finale, danced on the points. But at one venue, the boards of the stage were loose, and down he fell, tearing his Achilles tendon, which wrecked his act for some time. There were compensations, however, while playing on military bases. After the show, the performers were often welcomed into the officers' mess, where they enjoyed a rare bit of luxury: warmth, a well-served meal, and perhaps a glass of wine.

The value of the experience of working for ENSA varied. For those who were well established and already popular, participation offered an opportunity to contribute to the war effort and maintain public standing. For some at the beginnings of their careers, ENSA offered an opportunity to show off talent. Ivy Benson certainly benefited from the exposure offered by the many wartime gigs she did with ENSA, which in turn led to her great popularity with soldiers, sailors, and airmen. Others who had been minor entertainers before the war developed their skills while in ENSA, going on to enjoy major post-war careers. Singer Vera Lynn and comedians Spike Milligan and Terry Thomas were such, and Benny Hill worked for ENSA's successor, CSE—Combined Services Entertainment—right at the end of the war. Some artists—like comedian Tommy Trinder, who perhaps had not yet thought about a career in entertainment—were "discovered" while performing for ENSA. But perhaps for many, working with ENSA offered a chance to perform as professional entertainers for the first time in their lives and be paid relatively well at ten pounds per week (about £564 today, not far off the basic pay in a London West End theater). They had opportunities to travel and to work with established performers, opportunities that never would have emerged had it not been for the work of ENSA.

Ivy and her band contributed hugely to the war effort by entertaining the troops at home and abroad. Working for ENSA, and after the war with CSE, they built up a loyal following. The base of their popularity for many years after the war was the way in which they had represented the unquenchable spirit of performers at that time, the way in which women had worked hard in difficult situations to offer entertainment and a little glamor to both servicemen and workers on the home front. The opportunities that the war offered and that Ivy had grasped in 1939 stood her in good stead for another four decades as a bandleader.

At the end of the war, while established performers resumed their careers and some new performers went on to have successful careers in the theater, film, and television, most of those who had worked for ENSA quietly went back to their civilian lives. Wartime entertainment provided many happy memories of the time that they were, just for a short time, in great demand.

6

BATTLE OF THE SAXES

The year 1943 developed into a significant one for the Benson band. Because of the rapidly declining number of male musicians, the BBC had instead relied on men over forty-one who had not then been conscripted. Some conscientious objectors were available to play, but the BBC was reluctant to use them to broadcast in fear of public criticism, and this depleted the pool of talent even further. Women filled the gap. Ivy and her band were given increasing amounts of airtime until in January of that year, thanks again to Jack Hylton, an admirer and friend, Ivy was contracted as one of the BBC's resident bands.

All the well-known bands coveted such an opportunity, and Ivy's appointment by the BBC made her the target of much venom from male contemporaries. Some were apoplectic. Many were jealous of her success. "What is the only sight less sexy than a man playing a trombone?" asked a classic joke of the time. Answer, "A girl playing a trombone." A pretty weak joke, but the male chauvinists in the business found it difficult to get their heads around an all-girl orchestra, particularly one that played well. At various times the gender, the sexuality, and the morals of the women Ivy hired were raised as reasons to prevent their acceptance as a band: they were men in drag, they were all lesbians, they were prostitutes. Up until this point, most male bandleaders had regarded Ivy's ensemble as something of a novelty, but now that she had plenty of bookings and a growing number of fans, they deeply resented her.

Though Ivy's band could play most kinds of genre music, including the repertoire of the popular Glenn Miller, and though they had the grudging acceptance of some bandleaders that the band played well, were thoroughly rehearsed, and were not at all freakish, some considered anything that she and her band did was done better by men. They didn't mind her having the little bookings but didn't like her getting a plum job. Some of them really didn't want to know her; they hated her guts. Billy Ternent was particularly hostile, although Jack Hylton, always a good friend, was supportive, as was bandleader Joe Loss. There was even a campaign of dirty tricks. One arranger deliberately put wrong notes in their music scores, and the Musicians' Union sent an angry delegation to the BBC to complain about Ivy's appointment. It became known as the Battle of the Saxes. But the BBC decided that Ivy's band deserved their place and refused any suggestions that she should be fired. The reviews for the first broadcast were savage, but Ivy's band continued to play and win enthusiastic support from their listeners.

The BBC bands were by then based in Bristol, in the southwest of England, because of the London bombing, and each band took its turn so that the BBC could maintain continual broadcasting. Because of the time zone differences in some of the countries where troops were stationed, the bands were called in at all hours to play, sometimes twelve times a week. As it was radio, they couldn't be seen, so some of Ivy's girls played in pajamas and hairnets. Ivy remembered one girl, Lillian Kelly, in her nightclothes and curlers, weeping profusely at the piano, because her husband was in the Seventh Army and had been posted overseas. Ivy had to cheer her up to get her through the session. The studios were underground, and the girls had to learn firefighting and take their turns clambering up onto the roof with their tin helmets and equipment. They thought it was great fun and a change from playing in the band. Pay was two hundred pounds a week for a twenty-four-piece band, union rate at the time, and from this Ivy had to pay the girls and all expenses. A bed with a coal fire, breakfast, and a hot supper cost about one pound five shillings a week. But at least for the BBC broadcasts Ivy didn't have to worry about the expense of stage outfits; pajamas were fine. But as the war progressed, with the increasing rationing of clothes, obtaining enough coupons required all her inventiveness.

Ivy, who did everything for the band herself, having no backers or managers at that time, recalled later that it was "really tough, and at times I wanted to pack it in because it worried me—it really did." But she must not have shown her discomfort to her girls. Joyce Terry, a singer in Ivy's band from 1943, recalled, "Men tried to put us down, but we wouldn't have it, and Ivy wouldn't have it. She thought there wasn't anything we couldn't do. We were going all 'round the country, living wonderful lives. Not depending on any men. We were earning our own living, doing what we wanted to do—and doing it very well, too."

The year continued to be a good one for Ivy. The band even appeared in a feature film for British National Studios, *The Dummy Talks*. It is a strange story, about the murder of a ventriloquist that takes place during a variety performance at the Empire Theatre. A dwarf is then sent undercover as the dummy. The film starred famous actors Jack Warner and Claude Hulbert, and Ivy played herself in a small speaking role. One reviewer noted, "a number of genuine variety acts add a flavour of the period, although they provide rather too much of the film's running time." Another commented that the film was "a weird but engaging second feature." It was never going to be one of the main features in a cinema program, which at the time typically consisted of two films, trailers for future films, cartoons, and a newsreel. In wartime, everyone relied on the newsreels to keep up visually with what was happening, even though a new edition only came out at weekly intervals, changing with the cinema's program. *The Dummy Talks* would be a B film, which was not an official category but indicated it was of a lesser quality than the main A-rated film. But despite the fact that the film is not memorable, that Ivy's band was the one chosen to appear on screen indicated her high visibility on the wartime music scene.

The type of music that Ivy chose to play contributed to her success and sustained her appeal after the war ended. By the early 1940s, levels of patriotism had grown, British music was thought desirable, and the American style of swing was becoming less popular. Some British bands—for example, Geraldo's—were seen as pseudo-American and lost support from the BBC. Glenn Miller's music was still in high demand, however, and in the summer of 1944, Miller took his fifty-piece Army Air Force Band on a very successful tour in England, giving eight hundred performances. While there, he recorded at EMI-owned Abbey Road Studios. He spent his last night in England near Bedford. On the morning of December 15, 1944, Miller took a flight en route to Paris; he'd wanted to finalize arrangements to move his entire band there in the near future. The plane disappeared over the English Channel, and he was presumed dead. Though his music lives on, the authentic sound of Miller's band was lost forever.

In October of 1943, Ivy plus the rhythm and strings section of her orchestra made their first records for EMI at their Abbey Road studios. The brass section was not used because of poor intonation. This was the first of only three recording sessions that Ivy made as Ivy Benson and Her All Girls Band, Ivy playing alto clarinet with Kay Yorston on vocals. The recorded numbers were mainly popular sentimental wartime songs, expressing the feelings of young men and women facing long separations. The "Home Coming Waltz," "We Mustn't Say Goodbye," and "I'm Getting Sentimental Over You" appear on the record and were staples too of the band's stage appearances. The thought of a large number of attractive women, obviously of the age likely to be missing husbands, sweethearts, and brothers must have added to the poignancy of the music. There were other wartime recordings, in November 1943 and in January 1944. But without the trumpets, horns, and trombones, the sound on the records, while pleasing, does not show her band's full range. The band in full throat with the brasses blaring can be heard best on filmed archive recordings from live performances.

Preferred British band music at that time mainly used 6/8 time—waltzes or slow swing tunes—and Ivy was easily able to adapt to what the public wanted. Her numbers, sung by female vocalists, most often at that time Kay Yorston or Rita Williams, expressed a yearning to be reunited with loved ones away from home. "I'm Sending My Blessings" was a prayer for a time when a young man serving abroad would once again be in his girl's arms, with her blessing sent by a bird, flying overseas:

> A bluebird sings, then spreads its wings
> And flies from me to you.

And hearing Ivy's band play "I'm in the Mood for Love" encouraged couples, likely to be parted at any time, to dance more closely together and forget the morrow. Dance band songs of the day, usually sung by attractive young vocalists, probably contributed to any number of hasty pairings and wartime marriages.

> I'm in the mood for love
> Simply because you're near me.

Blessings and bluebirds? Schmaltzy to modern ears they may be, but they made a great contribution to the morale of troops serving overseas. Lonely young men could feel assured that they were not forgotten and that the women at home were waiting for their return.

Many years later, in 1973, Ivy recalled to the *Jersey Evening Post* that she had once been asked to record an LP after the war. She'd picked a number of top session musicians to play with her, including singer Kathy Stobart, forming a twenty-five-piece orchestra to record a collection of numbers. But problems had arisen, and the record had seemed destined, she said, for a lengthy stay in the dark of the recording company's cellars. She'd forgot about it for years. Then one day she heard an LP of the identical set of numbers that had been released in America, recorded by, it said on the label, Mark Andrews and his orchestra. "It was us. Of that was no doubt," said Ivy. "Bandleaders know their own sound intimately. But I haven't done anything about it. I've always considered it a compliment, actually," she told the journalist with a wry smile, "that an all-girl band was classed good enough to become an all-male band on record."

The same month Ivy and her band recorded for EMI, Jack Hylton secured the band a twenty-two-week residency at the London Palladium, a top venue for variety performances. There they worked alongside top acts of the time, including comedians Max Miller and Jimmy James, piano duo Rawicz and Landauer, and singers Anne Ziegler and Webster Booth. They also performed as part of the Jazz Jamboree at the Stoll Theatre in London. The band had progressed from skepticism and sometimes outright ridicule to playing in prestigious venues around the United Kingdom.

However, Ivy and her musicians continued to experience some prejudice. According to Christina Baade, scholar of popular music and gender and media, the BBC's Overseas Entertainment Unit cut Ivy's sessions in half as part of an economizing mission and allowed her contract to expire in February 1944. It seems that such an economy drive did not apply to her male counterparts, as the BBC did not reduce any sessions of the other house bands, including those of Jack Payne and Billy Ternent. Even at this point, an all-women dance band was not considered the equal of its male counterparts.

Ivy's girls were glamorous and dressed like starlets on stage, often wearing matching gowns in bright fabrics. Glamor was important in wartime. Pinned to barracks walls, hung in submarines, and tucked into soldiers' pockets were calendars and posters printed with bright drawings of scantily clad, beautiful women, carefully designed by the US government as morale boosters, aimed at keeping the serviceman focused on doing his job for an all-American sweetheart back home, a girl worth fighting for. In America, adverts for female jazz musicians asked for a photograph from applicants. When remembering the time in later life, Ivy admitted that she too had been aware that men wanted to see attractive women, and although she didn't ask for a photograph when hiring, she preferred to employ pretty girls, ideally between eighteen and twenty-four, and glamorously decked out. But such glamour was hard to maintain in a large ensemble in wartime. Obtaining matching stage outfits for every band member was no small feat.

On June 1, 1941, clothes rationing had been introduced, which worked by allocating each type of clothing item a points value that varied according to how much material and labor went into its manufacture. Eleven coupons were needed for a dress, two for a pair of stockings, five for a pair of women's shoes. When buying new clothes, the shopper had to hand over coupons with a points value as well as money. Every adult was initially given an allocation of sixty-six points to last one year, but this allocation shrank as the war progressed, and at its lowest, from September 1945 to April 30, 1946, only twenty-four coupons were issued, effectively allowing the shopper only three coupons a month. Although there were special provisions for some people, including theatrical performers, stage costumes were hard to fund, especially in large numbers. In wartime Britain it had become unfashionable to be seen wearing clothes that were obviously showy, yet women were frequently implored to not let standards slip too far, as that could be a sign of low morale, which the government wanted to guard against. This was a major factor in the decision to continue the manufacture of cosmetics, though in much-reduced quantity. The major cosmetics houses created imaginative patriotic packaging. There were powder puffs in the shape of military caps. Shades of lipstick were given military names: Lips in Uniform by Tangee and Helena Rubinstein's uncompromising Regimental Red lipstick to name just two.

But as the war progressed, and as supply ships were sunk, factories bombed, and ingredients repurposed into armaments, production slowed to a trickle, and people started to run out of many things, including makeup. Any items that were for sale attracted the enormous purchase tax levied on all luxury goods. Eventually it became impossible to buy whole makeup items at all. Metal was unavailable for such frivolous purposes as lipstick cases or compacts, and soon only powder without a puff or occasionally lipstick refills were available and very expensive. Improvising makeup and having nice hairstyles took on an increased importance, and many women went to great lengths to still feel well-dressed and stylish even if their clothes were last season's, their stockings darned, and their accessories homemade. Women found creative ways around shortages, with beetroot juice used for a splash of lip color, boot polish passing for mascara, gravy browning rubbed in to simulate stockings, and pencil lines drawn up the backs of legs as seams. They resorted to smoothing Vaseline on their eyelids for shine and melting down the stubs of old lipsticks.

Second-hand clothing was available without coupons, however, and warm fur coats were quite easily obtained. It is strange to our modern eyes to see photographs of bleak wartime streets with women dressed in furs. There is even a press photo of the young Ursula Wood (later to be Mrs. Vaughan Williams) pushing her coal allowance home in a wheelbarrow while wearing a fur coat. Dress material as well as off-the-peg clothing was rationed by coupon, but curtain material was not, so that was often used for stage clothes; the heavier materials were more durable when costumes had to be used frequently before replacement. Looking after the costumes was a real headache, as such materials were much harder to care for than those available today. There was no polyester or crease-free stretchy fabric, and brocade, taffeta, satins, and velvet, which often looked good on stage, were produced from different fibers than modern ones. They needed careful laundering and were easily scorched if not ironed very carefully, a headache for performers on tour. Luxury fabrics were rare and very expensive, so hard-wearing parachute silk was highly prized for underwear, nightclothes, and wedding dresses. On one occasion, Ivy was helped out by some GIs who had gotten hold of a relatively large amount of the silk for her; she was able to have sixteen dresses made out of it. She became inventive about changing the trimmings to give the impression of new dresses. Nylons too were easily snagged, and the provision of these too came courtesy of the Americans. When performing at bases abroad with ENSA, the girls could wear uniforms on stage, and of course alluring costumes were not necessary when the band played on the radio. But wherever possible, Ivy's band did their best to provide both glamour and professional entertainment in an uncertain world.

A provincial tour followed the London Palladium, which included the Belle Vue Ballroom in Manchester. Ivy was taken ill during that period and needed surgery. She left a skeleton band of nine musicians in the charge of Norma Cameron, her alto sax player. Toni (Jessie) Beale, the trumpet player in the band, recalls Ivy's health struggles and how the band members were parceled out more than once to keep them in work until Ivy returned after convalescence. Toni played at a circus. It was probably at this time that Ivy lost one of her kidneys, which limited the immunizations she could tolerate. Those required for travel in Asia would not be available to her in the future. At that time she had no real plans to work abroad. But this changed within months, when she began what was to be the beginning of a life of touring.

The band was by now immensely popular with the troops and continually received top rating on the War Office charts of entertainers. Ivy received three hundred letters a week from British servicemen stationed abroad. The band spent so much time entertaining the troops that they became known as the Services Sweetheart Orchestra. It was about this time that Ivy adopted a signature tune; her earlier recordings don't feature the number that would become so associated with her. The story is that the editor of one of the big music weeklies of the time approached her and asked if he could write her biography. He wanted to call it by the less-than-catchy title *Lady Be Goodman*, in reference to the influence Benny Goodman had on her music. The book was never written, but the encounter gave her the idea to choose Lester Young's "Lady Be Good" for her signature tune, and thereafter a gig was not complete without it.

When the Ivy Benson All Girls Band struck up their theme tune, many of the service personnel who packed their shows in the 1940s wished fervently that the entrancing musicians would be anything but good once they came off stage. The persuasive lyrics appealed to women to be kind to servicemen far from home and very lonely. And some of Ivy's girls, to Ivy's constant disappointment, responded to their young suitors, leaving Ivy to seek yet another recruit to fill the gap.

> Oh, sweet and lovely lady, be good
> Oh, lady, be good to me.

But perhaps more often the title acted as a reminder to Ivy's girls of the good behavior she expected of them when they left the stage to face the adulation of hundreds of lonely young men.

7

THE WARTIME "GIRLS"

It soon became more and more difficult for Ivy to maintain a full lineup. There had not been many female band musicians visible before the war, but suddenly they were in demand. Good instrumentalists were in short supply. Mixed bands became more common, and Ivy wasn't the only woman running an all-girl band. Edna Croudson, Blanche Coleman, Gloria Gaye, and Dorothy Marno all led such bands, although none of them proved to be as enduring as Ivy Benson's.

To some extent, women were freer than they had been. Many men were fully occupied in the forces or in reserved occupations, so single women or those with no children, newly released from domestic expectations, were required to contribute to the war effort. But although there were more women available for work, there was no large pool of talented women looking for jobs as musicians, especially those who were used to playing the music that would ensure Ivy's band would be hired. So Ivy set about recruiting musicians with such potential, knowing that she would have to coach them into being the players she needed.

The north of England, particularly the counties of Yorkshire and Lancashire, was a main source of good women players, especially trumpeters and saxophonists. They had often played alongside fathers and brothers in the brass bands associated with collieries and other heavy industries, such as the famous Black Dyke Mills Band, the Fairey

Aviation Works Band, and Fodens Motor Works Band. The dads often trained their children to follow in their footsteps, and these brass bands offered opportunities for girls to play with men and boys on equal terms, opportunities not easily available to women musicians in the predominantly male environment of prewar dance bands.

Ivy Benson's friend Harry Mortimer knew many of the northern brass bands, some of which he conducted, and he was able to act as scout, recommending promising female players to Ivy. Like her, Harry came from Yorkshire. He was a well-respected composer and conductor who specialized in brass band music and conducted many successful brass bands, including the Black Dyke Mills Band. He was regarded as one of the world's best cornet players. Before the war, he had been a soloist with the Hallé Orchestra in Manchester, with the Royal Liverpool Philharmonic Orchestra, and with the BBC Northern Orchestra. He lectured and taught trumpet at the Royal Northern College of Music in Manchester. Ivy trusted Harry's judgment in recommending up-and-coming female brass instrumentalists who wanted a professional career. Each musician Harry suggested to Ivy would then be invited to audition for her. Many won a place in the band and started immediately.

Sometimes Ivy had no choice as to who played in her band. The female ENSA recruits from the entertainment industry who were not famous were regarded in the same way as any other women required to do patriotic war work and were allocated to wherever their services were needed. In 1944, Josephine Glover, sixteen years old and still at school, auditioned for ENSA first in Manchester and then at Drury Lane in London. She already played the accordion, piano, and saxophone in an amateur dance band. When she was on her way back from the audition on the train from London to Manchester, she sat in a packed compartment full of soldiers. One of them noticed her accordion case on the luggage rack and insisted she play for them. She accompanied their singing all the way home to Manchester. A few days later she was accepted by ENSA, allowed to leave school, and assigned to Ivy Benson's all-girl band. But she was there only a few months when she was transferred to a Scottish group, the Bluebells of Scotland, and played with them until the end of the war. Ivy was not given the option of retaining her and was left with yet another seat to fill.

Ivy kept her own ears open for promising instrumentalists. In 1940, for example, she heard the young Gracie Cole playing cornet on a broadcast of brass band music. Impressed by the sound, Ivy wrote from Manchester where the band was playing at the Ritz to invite Yorkshire-based Gracie to join the band on trumpet. Gracie was only sixteen, and her father thought her too young to leave home, particularly during wartime. Gracie herself did not want to leave her beloved brass band world or change from cornet to trumpet at the time. She was broadcasting with well-known brass bands such as Fodens and the Grimethorpe Colliery Band, as well as playing piano and singing with a dance band in Mexborough, Yorkshire. She was much in demand as a musician and had many offers.

Two years later, in 1942, Gracie Cole became the first woman to compete for the Alexander Owen Olivier Memorial Scholarship and won by an unprecedented twenty-one-point margin. Now that she was eighteen, her father decided she was old enough to tour with a band, but he chose Gloria Gaye's band rather than Ivy's. Gracie played cornet and trumpet with Gloria for eighteen months, touring theaters in the United Kingdom and working for ENSA and then with Rudy Starita's All Girl Band. Ivy had to wait until 1945 to secure Gracie for her own band, but secure her she did. Gracie Cole stayed with Ivy for five years.

One of the early recruits to the band, however, was not from the North but did have a musical background similar to Ivy's. Norma Cameron was born in Kent and had been taught music by her father. At eight she had started to learn the piano, violin, and mandolin, but by eleven, forced to make a choice by her father, she chose to play a C-melody saxophone. She started her performing life accompanying her banjo-playing father at concerts in hotels, and as she got older, she played gigs with local bands. In September 1943, Norma received a telegram from Ivy Benson asking if she was interested in joining her in Bristol, where the band was under contract for the BBC. As usual, there was no formal audition; Norma was handed a tenor sax, not her usual instrument, and sat in on the rehearsal. Obviously satisfied by what she heard, Ivy asked Norma to play in the broadcast that night. Norma stayed with the band throughout the war until 1947, even deputizing for the bandleader at the Belle Vue Ballroom in Manchester in 1945 when Ivy was taken ill. From 1947 to 1955, Norma Cameron spent time on and off with Ivy, playing lead alto sax. Like many women in the band, she later forged her own career in music, playing for other bandleaders and forming her own six-piece group.

But perhaps the most unlikely member of the wartime band was Edith Whitley, who joined at the age of fifty-one, in 1942. The majority of Ivy's players were in their teens and twenties, and many of the stories that Ivy told about traveling with the band relate to losing her girls to marriage with soldiers and trying to simultaneously be boss, coach, and surrogate mother to the very young ones. This wasn't a problem with Edith, who was twenty years older than her employer when she became one of Ivy's "girls." She had seen life and experienced things that none of the others could have, including World War I as an adult. Although Edith had been born in Bradford, Yorkshire, in 1889, she and her husband had emigrated to Canada in 1909 with their small daughter. Two baby boys were born there, but both died. Her husband's job fell through, and, as the couple could not afford the fare for both of them to return to England, a pregnant Edith returned to her family in Bradford, alone, where she had her fourth child. Her husband eventually returned to the family in 1914, but despite being declared unfit for early service in World War I, he responded to the Army's later decision to take anyone who could walk and joined up in 1917. He was injured during a battle in France and had to have a leg amputated. Like many others in that terrible war, he could not be given the medical care he needed near the battlefield and, tragically, died of shock and pneumonia. Edith was left a widow with two small children to support. She decided that, as she had some musical talent, she would apply for a scholarship. She was successful, and studied with the famous cellist Karl Fuchs. She mastered the cello and also the saxophone and harp and played professionally to keep the family. Soon after the outbreak of World War II, and no longer with young children, she heard of Ivy Benson's All Girl Band, applied for an audition, and was accepted. She played cello and saxophone with the band from 1942 to 1946.

But many of Ivy's players were very young. Until 1944, all British children were required to remain in school until at least the age of fourteen, and some of the girls Ivy recruited were only fifteen but looked older on stage. These girls had their audiences queuing for dates as well as for dancing. Ivy had to play employer, musical coach, and, as one of the girls reported, "the mother hen looking after her young." She was a strict but fair boss, but with such a large group of young girls to control and take responsibility for, she needed to use both the gentle and the strict sides of her nature.

If recruitment was a problem, retention was an even greater one, and intractable. It was a constant battle to keep a full lineup of musicians. Ivy knew that society thought women should be wives and mothers, and that what she offered her players did not fit into those strictures. The band was constantly on the move; at first to gigs and bases around Britain, but later in Europe and further afield. Ivy was reluctant to employ married women, as inevitably they wanted to be free when their husbands were on leave from the forces. But there were exceptions. With their men at war, some wives without children took advantage of the wartime need for entertainers and joined bands and groups as their contribution to the war effort. One such was Toni (Jessie) Beale, already an established trumpeter. Just before the war she and her husband had moved in with her parents to a house on the island of Jersey to be safe, they thought, from the coming conflict. Ironically, this would not be the case, as her parents would later be interned when Germany occupied the Channel Islands in 1940. Toni was running a women's band in Saint Helier in Jersey when she received a job offer from Coventry; Dorothy Holbrook wanted Toni to join her Harmony

Hussars on tour. Then war broke out, and her plans had to change. Jim, Toni's husband, was sent to Tidworth Camp in Wiltshire, where she decided to join him until he moved overseas. They lived off the base in nearby digs, and Jim formed a camp band, which included Toni as the only woman. As an able bugler, she was trusted to blow reveille some mornings. One day one of the officers showed her an advertisement that had appeared that morning in various papers. Ivy Benson, with her keen awareness of who the good women musicians were, needed an experienced trumpeter for an ENSA tour that was starting soon. She was advertising specifically for Toni. The advertisements stated that she "was last known to be near her husband at Tidworth." Toni and Jim talked it over, and as he was likely to be posted abroad, Toni joined Ivy and stayed with her throughout the war.

By her own admission, Ivy sought ideally to recruit attractive young women, and, according to 1950s band member Nora Coward (née Lord), Ivy spent a lot of her money on making the band alluring. This could not help but become a recipe for retention difficulties. The band traveled around the country to bases full of lonely and virile young men as well as playing to packed dance halls of servicemen on leave. The heightened awareness of danger as bombs fell and the likelihood of troops going overseas meant that relationships developed quickly. There was little time to be lost, and it was essential to seize the moments of pleasure. Many of Ivy's girls left her to be with their partners before they went away and sometimes to marry quickly.

And then there were the Americans. They were here and weren't leaving any time soon.

8

OVERPAID, OVERSEXED, AND OVER HERE

It wasn't just British servicemen who loved Ivy's band. Overseas service personnel flocked to hear them too. Canadians, as members of British Commonwealth troops, had been stationed in the south of England since 1939, mostly in Aldershot, but from 1942 onward there were hordes of young men arriving from America, stationed on military bases throughout the United Kingdom. Attractive and friendly, they were more than ready to fill the gap left by absent British soldiers and were to prove a constant problem for Ivy. Many of her musicians could not resist their offers of marriage, sometimes within twenty-four hours of meeting. A whole band section went missing on one tour, and even as late as 1968 Ivy was reporting losing instrumentalists to GIs. There always seemed to be empty places on stage to fill. And the attraction of American servicemen was not only a professional problem. It was to affect her personal life directly too.

In the early 1940s, while Britain resounded to bombing and its people coped with increasing shortages and privations, there were no major changes felt across the Atlantic by American citizens. However, at that time it was not yet clear what role Americans might play in that war. Although many were sympathetic to the Allies, there were deep political divisions in the United States about any direct involvement in the war. The public did not know whether members of their family would be required to fight. However, after the Japanese bombing of Pearl Harbor on December 7, 1941, the threat of war became real.

The United States formally entered into World War II on the next day. Patriotism increased exponentially. The country mobilized with civilian defense, war bond drives, the expansion of defense industries, and the establishment of military training camps. The conscription of soldiers began. The Office of War Information attempted to encourage such patriotism and to shape popular belief and culture through its information program. Millions of people moved away from their homes, twelve million for military service and fifteen million to work in the new industries that demanded their skills.

The first GIs landed on Britain's shores in 1942 and started establishing bases. Technically speaking, the United States had no bases in Britain in World War II but rented them from the Royal Air Force. But in reality, many of them were built to US Army Air Forces specification and were exclusively occupied by American personnel. Nearly 90 percent of all US bases in the United Kingdom were in the southeastern corner of England, from which airmen flew hazardous daylight raids over Europe. Transport, training, and fighter squadrons were stationed in over seventy bases spread out over the entire country, but most of stations that flew the Boeing B-17 Flying Fortress bombers were clustered in East Anglia and the East Midlands in counties such as Norfolk, Suffolk, and Lincolnshire. These counties were flat, had low population density, and were a short flying distance from the European heartland.

If film stars, singers, and girl bands represented female glamour in 1942, then the GIs represented its male counterpart. The British soldiers in their rough wool serge khaki uniforms, a color that does little for most northern European complexions, were no match sartorially for the Americans in their smart lightweight outfits and shoes and with their caps worn at a jaunty angle. Although they were not all like the American heartthrobs seen on screen, these GIs were generally larger in physique and had better teeth than their less-well-fed British counterparts. They also smelled better, having access to aftershave and deodorants, unavailable to most Brits. Their wearing of rings, wrist-watches, and neck chains led to accusations of effeminacy from some British men, but there was no doubt that as far as British girls were concerned, the Americans were seen as a better prize. And, of course, they were "over here," when many young men from the villages and small towns where there were bases were serving overseas.

GIs were reportedly very generous. With average salaries more than five times that of a British soldier and no living expenses to worry about, there was plenty of time and money for parties. They also got paid monthly, so when pay day arrived, they would be seen with wads of notes they were happy to spend on hospitality off base. Apart from providing desirable men, the American bases were also a source of commodities long missing from British shops or severely rationed. Sweets, chocolate, tinned fruit, meat, coffee, cheese, and sugar for the family would often be used as part of the wooing of young women. Nylon stockings, something British women had almost forgotten, were not in the base stores but could be posted from the United States, often by relatives and friends who were careful not to arouse the suspicions of girlfriends back home. The base also provided condoms, almost impossible to find in the United Kingdom. Many people had never seen them. On at least one occasion, children found unused prophylactics and, thinking they were balloons, blew them up and strung them up in the street—to the horror of their mothers.

Despite a common language, the two nations quickly noticed differences. The GIs were frequently described as "overpaid, oversexed, and over here." The GIs retorted that the British were "underpaid, undersexed, and under Eisenhower." British women reported that the Americans had odd eating habits, flaunted their money, and could be boisterous and brash. They were often direct in their approach. One GI veteran recalled, "We would crash their parties, drink their beer, flirt with their women." They constantly chewed gum and paid minimum regard to military etiquette and rules, giving civilians lifts in military vehicles and allowing inquisitive schoolboys into security areas on the base. Relaxed and breezy, they greeted civilians, depending on age and gender, with "Hi, honey!" Howdy, Pop!" "Hiya, kids!" But they were a breath of fresh air in the dismal days of war, and many were invited into the homes of people, especially at Christmas, and maybe filled the gap left by a brother or son for a short time.

The US Office of War Information distributed publications to its servicemen detailing the culture in Britain and how American personnel should behave to avoid misunderstandings. For the same reason, the British Army Bureau of Current Affairs published a series of pamphlets as briefs intended for use by British officers for talks with their men. A number of these were about the differences between the British and Americans. In "Meet the Americans," Professor W. J. Hinton explained that despite the shared language, Americans were not a kind of Englishman and went on to outline how America evolved as a country and how the different traditions, manners, and vagaries of domestic life had developed. For example, he explained that American homes had many labor-saving devices and were much warmer than British houses at the time. "Remember this when your poor American friend shivers in the damp cold of the English winter, or grumbles at the absence of ice and the presence of warm beer. His sufferings are real, and he may express them with warmth proportionate to his discomfort. Don't be touchy if he takes a poor view of your home in consequence."

Perhaps most relevant to the way in which the GIs attracted women, including many of Ivy's band members, is a pamphlet published in 1944, written by distinguished American anthropologist Margaret Mead. The section on "Boy Meets Girl" is particularly revealing. At that time in America, Mead explained, American men and boys enjoyed the company of girls and women more that the British did. British boys didn't go out with girls unless they had what one British boy described to Mead as "an ulterior motive." If they just wanted to spend a pleasant evening out, they spent it with other boys. Many British men and women had been to single-sex secondary schools, but even when boys and girls were educated together, they still acted as though they were at separate schools. Quite differently, Mead observed, American boys and girls usually went to co-ed schools and started having dates with each other in their early teens, long before they were emotionally mature enough to be interested in each other for any reasons really connected with sex. She explained that there was a "well-established ritual of refusal." The boy proves he is popular by asking for a lot of favors, by starting right out pretending that he expects the girl to fall into his arms. The girl, to prove she is popular too, refuses him most or all of the favors he asks for. There is a lot of banter and joking. This game is quite different from being in love and is confusing to British girls who have no practice in the game of wisecracking. According to Mead, some British girls are insulted by the speed and assurance of the American's approach and turn chilly. But some of them take his words, which sound like wooing, for real wooing and give him a kiss with a warmth that surprises him. Some of them think the American is proposing and take him home to father. Mead explained to her intended British wartime audience that Americans start a relationship quickly, telling the other person everything about themselves but then taking it more slowly than the British. Standards of familiarity too were confusing, Mead explained. In America, men naturally take a girl's arm. In Britain, if a girl yields her arm and is seen publicly arm-in-arm with an American, she may regard herself as practically engaged, whereas the American's intention was merely courtesy. These and many other important differences in courting rituals may explain some of the very fast relationships that developed between American servicemen and British women. And some of the misunderstandings!

Over seventy thousand British women married Americans stationed in Britain and sailed across the Atlantic to new lives when the war ended. Most of the marriages survived, but some did not, the women realizing that, once home, the glamorous GI they had married was not who they'd thought he was. As the war moved toward its conclusion in 1945, thousands of brides and children sailed on big ships to America. In January that year, the *Daily Sketch* reported that the SS

Argentina was en route to the United States with thousands of wives and children of US servicemen, and 1,400 others were collecting at the Bournemouth reception center, ready to sail on the *Queen Mary* the following week. But already there was some two-way traffic. The same article reported that twenty disillusioned wives had returned from the United States. One girl said that her American soldier husband had told her that he owned a restaurant employing thirty waiters and a fifteen-piece orchestra. The restaurant had turned out to be a snack bar, and she was expected to be his chief cook and bottle washer. But the number of returners was a tiny proportion of those who left Britain, and the vast majority adjusted to their new homes in the United States and made good lives for themselves and their children.

Dancing to bands was the way in which many couples met, and of course the American servicemen were keen to dance. They enjoyed jazz and swing music, jukeboxes, and the jitterbug dance routines that became incorporated into band music when the GIs came to Britain. However, although American servicemen enjoyed access to much the same music as their British counterparts, they had much more experience of women jazz musicians. Like Britain, America had responded to its wartime footing and the need to provide entertainment for the troops and defense workers by filling the dance band shortage with women bands. But unlike many British bands, including Ivy's, these bands were not newly formed to take advantage of wartime needs. The American women who scrambled from one one-night gig to another during the war years were the same women who had "cut their teeth performing in all-girl bands in vaudeville and tent shows, dance halls, ballrooms, carnivals, and theaters a decade earlier." There were many all-women bands in America, and some were remembered as wartime phenomena. But, in fact, many of the most famous all-women bands, including those of Ina Ray Hutton and Rita Rio, actually disbanded before the US involvement in World War II, and many bands that did entertain during the war years such as the International Sweethearts of Rhythm and Phil Spitalny's Hour of Charm Orchestra had been established long before 1941. Because of the acceptance of women as band instrumentalists, the American all-women bands were not reviled by male bandleaders in the same way as Ivy's band. But, nevertheless, they were still regarded, much to their annoyance, as "Swing Shift Maisies," 1940s American slang for temporary substitutes for the "real" workers—the men—who were off in combat.

Americans arriving in Britain in preparation for active service were therefore used to women on bandstands. They had been on military bases in their own country where all-women bands had entertained. There were far fewer such bands to be seen in Britain. The American servicemen had no nervousness in approaching an attractive member of Ivy's band and beginning a relationship with her. Many of Ivy's musicians fell for the charms of American servicemen, and Ivy became resigned to, although never happy with, the loss of many good musicians and the constant need to replace them.

9

LIVING THROUGH HISTORY

In the spring of 1945, Ivy's band was visiting British bases in northern Germany with ENSA, helping entertain the troops. The war in Europe was slowly but surely coming to an end. In the south of Germany, US troops aimed to reach the northern entrances to the Alps before the Germans. They advanced swiftly and with very few casualties. Their opponents, short of experienced soldiers and materials, could do little to resist other than attempt to delay the US advance during the day, retreating by night. However, in the northeastern part of Germany it was a different story. Both the Russians and the Germans suffered heavy casualties as the Russians fought their way toward Berlin against intense opposition as the German war machine sought to protect its heart. The British and Canadians were advancing through the northwest of Germany. By mid-April, Ivy and her band were on tour and had arrived at a military base at Celle, about fifteen miles from the town of Bergen in Lower Saxony. The young women would have had no idea, as they arrived at yet another location to cheer the troops, of how notorious the name Bergen–Belsen would become and that they would be present at a turning point of history.

The Bergen–Belsen concentration camp, the only one taken by the British, had just been liberated a few days earlier by the Canadians and the British Eleventh Armoured Division on April 15. When the Allies advanced on Bergen–Belsen in 1945, the German army had negotiated a truce and an exclusion zone around the camp to prevent the spread of typhus, which had broken out in the camp and, along with other diseases caused by overcrowding, lack of food, and inadequate sanitary conditions, had already caused the deaths of more than thirty-five thousand people since the start of the year. On April 11, Heinrich Himmler, Reichsführer-SS, agreed to have the camp handed over without a fight, and SS guards ordered prisoners to bury some of the dead.

The soldiers who reached the camp on April 15 were totally unprepared for what they found there. They discovered approximately sixty thousand prisoners inside, most of them half-starved and seriously ill, and another thirteen thousand corpses lying around the camp unburied, including that of the teenage Anne Frank, a German-born Jewish diarist. A Jewish victim of the Holocaust, she gained fame posthumously with the publication of *The Diary of a Young Girl*, in which she documented her life in hiding from 1942 to 1944 during the German occupation of the Netherlands. Her older sister, Margot, was there too, having died of typhus.

As word spread of what had been found in the death camp, the horror reverberated around the world. Mass graves were dug to hold up to five thousand corpses at a time. The former army guards from the SS were deliberately made to use their bare hands to bury the prisoners, many of whom had died of contagious diseases. The mass evacuation of the camp began on April 21. Prisoners with any hope of survival were moved to an emergency hospital, and British medical students responded to an appeal from the Ministry of Health to go to Germany and help treat the prisoners. Most of the details did not appear in the media until a few days after the liberation, when the first medical teams were beginning to arrive.

Accompanying the British Eleventh Armoured Division as they entered the camp that April was Richard Dimbleby, the BBC's first war correspondent. He was so shocked with what they found there but so determined that the world would know that he prepared a graphic description of what he saw. The BBC refused to broadcast his dispatch. He threatened to resign, and the BBC relented four days later.

He spoke quietly and simply of seeing many dead and dying people, the living lying with their heads against the corpses. He described the awful sight of a procession of emaciated people who milled around, unseeing, unable to move out of his way and with no hope of life. One sight, seared into his memory, was the sight of a woman screaming at a British sentry to give her milk for her child. She had thrust a tiny bundle into the soldier's arms and run off, crying terribly. When the soldier opened the bundle, he found that the baby had been dead for several days.

Dimbleby described that day at Belsen as the most horrible of his life.

As Ivy's band had arrived in Celle only a few days after the liberation, it is unlikely that, in the bustle of being on tour, they would have known much about the coverage of Bergen-Belsen in the British newspapers. Nor was it likely that their hosts at the British airbase would have wanted to emphasize their proximity to the camp or tell the women much about the horror. After all, the purpose of the long-planned band visit was to entertain and cheer the troops, who must have been shocked and very upset. The work schedule, preparation for the concerts, and hospitality of the air base, although low-key, would probably have occupied the young women for most of their time. But one sunny afternoon, two of them, older than most of the other band members, and always keen to benefit from the chance to see the new places that they visited and not stay confined to military bases, decided to look around the area. Unaware of how close they were to the horrors of the concentration camp, they set off for a walk.

Forty years after the event, one of those young women, Toni (Jessie) Beale, was interviewed about her time with Ivy Benson's band. An elderly lady by then, Beale found it difficult sometimes to remember events and people and to find words. The interviewer worked hard to keep her on subject, and there were many pauses. But the events of that long-ago day were etched so deeply in her memory that she was able to recall almost every moment of that afternoon without the slightest hesitation, and the tears came unbidden.

Beale and her bandmate had set off along the main road. Hearing the sound of a vehicle, they hitched a lift with a sergeant and a corporal, who, stopping for the young women and assuring them that they had not pinched the petrol but had saved it up, offered to take them to see the Belsen camp. Toni and her friend didn't really know what it was but agreed to go along for the ride. It was a sunny day, and the flat main road stretched ahead. In the distance they could just make out two figures, and as they got closer, they saw an injured German soldier and a nurse just outside the camp. They could see the tall watchtowers and the barbed wire, hung with skull and crossbone warnings. The sergeant said, "I'm going to speak to those people." The German nurse, who spoke English, told him that she had traveled all the way around the world and seen many things but "I have to come to my own place to see such horrors." The corporal took out a pack of cigarettes and offered it to the injured German. Jessie still remembered the look on his face, the fear of the British soldier mixed with surprise at the unexpected kindness.

They entered the camp, which was guarded by British soldiers, and were sprayed with a white powdered disinfectant, which covered all the surfaces as far as they could see. Told not to look to a building on the right, as there were people who "may not all be dead," the girls could not stop themselves. There they saw faces pressed against the window. (Jessie's account of this horror is given with absolute clarity but through apologetic tears.) Moving on, they saw evidence of the pits where the bodies had been buried by the British soldiers, each marked with a small cross, and the places where people had been burned alive. Sickened by what they had seen, they turned to go back. Just then, there was the sound of two approaching motorcycles, on each a Belgian soldier. One, a big burly man, wept uncontrollably as he stood contemplating the scene, "crying like a child." The other, who had some English, said "Forgive my *bruder*, but here is where my father and mother are buried."

In silence, the two young women went out of the camp and into the most peaceful sunny day.

Back at the Celle base, the band was invited to watch a football match, and there Jessie talked to the senior RAF officer, Wing Commander King, about the visit. He spoke of his intense anger at the people of Celle who claimed not to have known what was going on at the camp even though the baker and other tradesmen had taken food up to the camp daily for the Germans. In his fury, King had forced the townspeople out onto the streets, no matter how old, slow, or incapacitated, and shown them some of the skeletal survivors. The commander reported incredulously that there had been some laughter from a few of the onlookers. With the hindsight of many years, one wonders if this was the nervous reaction of people who were feeling their guilt and inadequacy rather than intended disrespect or something they found truly humorous. But the whole episode remained imprinted on Jessie's memory for the rest of her life.

In the same week that the Bergen-Belsen camp was liberated, Stalin unleashed Russia's army and air force with the objective of crushing German resistance and capturing Berlin. By prior agreement, the Allied armies (positioned approximately sixty miles to the west) had halted their advance on the city in order to give the Soviets a free hand. Eventually, after strong resistance and cruelties on both sides, the depleted German forces succumbed to overwhelming force. Fighting street-to-street and house-to-house, Russian troops blasted their way toward Hitler's chancellery in the city's center. On April 30, 1945, in his final hours, the *Führer* married his longtime mistress, Eva Braun, and then together they committed suicide. Germany's surrender, therefore, was authorized by Hitler's successor, Reichspräsident Karl Dönitz. The act of military surrender was signed on May 7 in Reims, France, and on May 8 in Berlin. That day, Victory in Europe Day marked the formal conclusion of Hitler's war. For many countries this was the end of six years of misery and suffering but also of much courage and endurance.

Celebrations erupted throughout the Western world. In the United Kingdom, more than one million people celebrated in the streets to mark the end of the European part of the war. In London, crowds massed in Trafalgar Square and up the Mall to Buckingham Palace, where King George VI and Queen Elizabeth, accompanied by Prime Minister Winston Churchill, appeared on the balcony of the palace before the cheering crowds. The teenage princesses Elizabeth and Margaret were allowed out of Buckingham Palace and went dancing at the Ritz, a rare relaxation of protocol. And elsewhere in the country, the crowds were equally exuberant, although the euphoria was mixed with sadness in families who had lost members to fighting or bombs and intense weariness after six years of hardship. On July 21, Churchill visited Berlin for the British Victory Parade, and there were celebrations to follow. Ivy's band, already playing in Lüneburg in a German theater taken over by the British, was invited personally by Field Marshal Montgomery to join the victory celebrations. They closed the theater and flew to Berlin. At Montgomery's insistence, too, the band was the first to entertain the troops in Berlin after it fell to the Allies.

On August 6, 1945, the United States, with the consent of the United Kingdom, dropped an atomic bomb on the Japanese city of Hiroshima, followed by a second on August 9 on Nagasaki. Six days later, this previously unthinkable attack, still debated to this day, caused Japan to surrender. Finally, the war was over.

10

THE SHOCK OF BERLIN: THE FIRST POSTWAR TOUR

Ivy's life of touring did not stop with the end of World War II. Many Allied troops were still stationed at home and abroad and needed entertainment. Her band traveled mostly under the auspices of ENSA until the end of 1945 and then with the body that replaced it, Combined Services Entertainment. By this time, Ivy was not managing the band alone. Her father, Digger Benson, was helping as home road manager. According to Gracie Cole, who had recently been recruited as a trumpeter, the girls liked Digger and respected him as a musician. But Ivy took full responsibility for her girls, particularly the young ones. Sometimes the band would socialize in the officers' club after a concert, and "Ivy would go to the piano, play for atmosphere and a few requests. Boys would dance with girls, but at a certain time she'd put her hat on and say, 'Okay, girls, we're ready!' She'd stand there and have us filing past like a roll call. There was no question of hanky-panky—she was very strict, especially with girls under sixteen."

In December 1945 Ivy's band went overseas for ENSA, an eight-week tour of British Army on the Rhine bases, starting at Ostend in Belgium. Sometimes in the evening after a show, Ivy on clarinet, Lena Kidd on tenor sax, and Gracie Cole on trumpet would pop into the local jazz club for a "blow" with local musicians. They couldn't always converse with their hosts, but "jazz is a universal language." And it was during this tour that Ivy and her band made a memorable live broadcast on Christmas Day 1945 from the British Forces Network studios in Hamburg directly after the king's speech. Trumpeter Gracie remembered the thrill of hearing "'Now we take you to the Garrison Theatre in Hamburg to join the Ivy Benson All Girls Orchestra,' because the whole nation was listening." There was no doubt that Ivy's band had been taken into the hearts of the people. But there were troubles still to come.

Just as the war ended, Ivy Benson and her band, now called the Ladies Dance Orchestra, was booked for the first postwar broadcasts on BBC television, the new medium that was growing in popularity. But in June 1946, and only forty-eight hours before the band was due to appear for the first time, the Stoll Theatre group, uncertain of the reactions this all-girl phenomenon would provoke, threatened to cancel Ivy's contracts with them. They would not allow her to play in their theaters if she signed with the BBC. Male bandleaders were beginning to return from the war and intended once again to dominate the band scene in Britain, so there was much more competition for work. Ivy couldn't risk signing the television contract. The band circuit became booked up, and even the BBC turned its back on her. The Association of Bandleaders closed ranks and said that she couldn't join. "Forget it," said Ivy. "I don't want to be in."

Ivy had a booking for Las Vegas for the band after the war and was delighted, but the American Federation of Musicians stopped her going. This was tit-for-tat because the equivalent British union hadn't allowed American bands into Britain. Individual conductors and musicians could perform but not whole bands. Later, when in 1954 the musicians' unions of both countries still had not reached agreement, the intrepid Ivy flew alone to America to try and persuade James Petrillo, head of the federation, to agree to a scheme for exchanging visits by orchestras from Britain and the United States. She appeared on television and conducted a women's band during her visit, but things did not immediately change. Just after the war, too, she had an offer from the Lido in Paris but couldn't go there either for similar reasons of union opposition.

There seemed to be a conspiracy against Ivy and her band. She was annoyed at all the barriers that seemed to be in her way. But true to form, the hurdles only made her more determined to succeed. She retaliated by taking the band on their first European tour to Berlin with ENSA, to play for the Allied troops. This proved to be a turning point in her fortunes, and that successful first visit was the start of regular tours postwar, many to US bases, which continued for many years. It also ensured her an audience for her music that many male bands would envy.

The immediate postwar period in Germany saw destroyed cities, and many people were displaced. The country had been divided up into four zones, each ruled by one of the Allied powers—Britain, the Soviet Union, the United States, and France. Berlin, the capital and perhaps the worst affected city, was in ruins. In accordance with an agreement signed by the Allies, the city—by then in the Soviet-controlled part of the country—was divided into four sectors and administered jointly by the four occupying powers. British and American troops were stationed in their respective parts of Berlin, and their bases were strategically placed in other regions of Germany.

The first tour by Ivy's band to Berlin under the auspices of ENSA was an eye-opener. To those young British women now finding themselves for the first time in postwar Europe, what they saw and experienced was new and sometimes horrifying. Their route took them from the Netherlands into Germany and finally to the city of Berlin. In The Hague they walked out in the streets a little, but there were a lot of official restrictions, and they had to be accompanied by a soldier. The lovely curved shop windows reminiscent of those in the West End of London had nothing in them except just one item apiece, to show what type of shop they had been prewar and what, perhaps, they hoped to be in a better future. One shop, which a few of the band entered, had just one shoe in the window, and a customer with a basket on the counter was trying to sell old shoes to buy food. The woman seemed ashamed at what she was reduced to and covered her basket when she saw the English girls. No one had anything. People were ill-shod, and those who had bicycles rode them with no tires. The people looked half-starved, and the visitors were shocked.

Crossing into Germany, however, they found another world. Jessie Beale was angry to see women in beautiful suits and leather shoes and Germans riding good bicycles. She was furious that it was so near a place where people had nothing. It was many miles before the group saw anything bad again. But then their transport entered Berlin.

What it must have been like to be such young women, some as young as seventeen and many who had not been out of Britain before, suddenly finding themselves in a Europe shattered by war can only be imagined. Although they were cushioned to some extent from postwar privations, often being entertained in well-equipped military bases, many of Ivy's ensemble would never forget what they saw at that time. Between bases and engagements, they traveled by road through Holland and Germany. Imprinted on Ivy's memory was a picture of wrecked houses in a snowy Cuxhaven at the mouth of the River Elbe in Lower Saxony, with the remains of half-eaten meals and abandoned half-packed suitcases. In Berlin, there were still piles of rubble everywhere and rows of building walls with collapsed interiors, the skeletons of a destroyed city. Palaces, museums, churches, monuments, and cultural sites had fallen victim to the bombs, and six hundred thousand apartments had been destroyed. When the Russians had arrived, only 2.8 million of the city's original population of 4.3 million were still living in the city. On May 29, 1945, all women between the ages of fifteen and sixty-five had been conscripted as *Trümmerfrauen*— rubble women—to clear the streets. In all, sixty thousand women worked to rebuild Berlin.

But the biggest problem that the Berliners had to face was the threat of starvation. German wartime ration cards were no longer valid. Any remaining rations were either used to feed Russian troops or stolen by hungry Germans. Two weeks earlier, on May 15, the Russians had introduced a new, five-tier ration-card system. The highest tier was reserved for intellectuals and artists (an interesting choice in light of later Soviet-era preferences and the persecution of such groups). Rubble women and manual workers received the second-tier card, which was more valuable to them than the twelve reichsmarks they received for cleaning up each thousand bricks. The lowest card, cynically nicknamed the cemetery ticket, was issued to housewives and the elderly. During this period, the average Berliner was around thirteen to twenty pounds underweight.

Those touring with Ivy's band at that time remembered the terrible living conditions. Elsie Ford, a bass player who worked with Ivy all through the war, recalled it vividly: "I remember when the band went to Berlin just after the war ended, and there wasn't a pane of glass in the windows of the place where we stayed. We couldn't drink any water; we couldn't even clean our teeth in it; it all had to be out of a bottle, because there were thirty thousand dead bodies under Berlin." There was little food to be had for civilians in the city. It was cold and snowy, and people were obviously very hungry. Although forbidden to give food to the Germans, Ivy and the girls were horrified to see children starving. They would collect up their meager breakfasts—sardines, bread, and tea—and sneak around the back streets to give them to the children.

One evening, Ivy's band attended an event at a house that before the war had been the home of Dr. Robert Ley, a prominent Nazi who had remained loyal to Hitler right up to the end and who had been known for his big spending, womanizing, and heavy drinking. Ley had freely embezzled funds from his party. Captured by the Americans in May 1945 after fleeing Berlin, he had been indicted at the Nuremberg trials and strangled himself in his cell three days later. He had owned a luxurious estate near Cologne, a string of villas in other cities, a fleet of cars, a private railway carriage, and large collections of art and of books. Some of these books were still in his Berlin house, and Ivy, accompanied by a Dutch liaison officer, was allowed to look at the collection but not touch. She admired two beautifully bound books, *The Memoirs of Casanova*. When the function was over, she went to collect her coat from the cloakroom. The Dutch officer was there and nonchalantly handed over the coat, which seemed very heavy. Forty years later, the two books were still on Ivy's bookshelves. "But after forty years, it really doesn't matter," she said.

There are amusing stories too. For example, Ivy and the band were the first English girls to enter Berlin and were much admired by all the young men serving there. Traveling from West Germany to the eastern sector of Berlin, they had to deal with the Russian guards, who were just young boys. Ivy showed her passport the wrong way up. The guard looked at it like that and nodded her through the checkpoint. Drummer Paula Pyke described the snow that day. "It was four feet deep, and Robey Buckley, who came from Australia, had never seen snow before and just rolled in it! We all started playing snowballs, and in the end the guards joined in!"

The Montague Burton Factory, Leeds, where Ivy started work

Ivy, the young saxophonist, with band

Wedding of bandleader Ivy Benson to Caryll Clark
at Caxton Hall, London

Basil Dean

Berlin in ruins, when Ivy and the band were there,
visiting military bases, 1945

Combined Services Entertainment
poster advertising Ivy's band on tour

Villa Marina on the Isle of Man,
where Ivy and her band performed
over many summer seasons

Ivy marries Top Sergeant Berthold
Brantley Calloway of the US Air
Force, September 1957

Wedding "guard of honor"

Ivy judging a children's talent
contest, July 1961

Three instrumentalists
in modern uniforms for
daytime playing during
the summer season, Isle
of Man, 1961

Poster for *Silver Lady*, Birmingham Repertory Theatre, with the real Ivy Benson band as the background, 1984

Program for *Silver Lady*, with Ivy as the background, 1984

Ivy rehearsing the *Silver Lady* band, 1984

Actor Polly Hemingway and Ivy, 1984

Polly Hemingway as Ivy, with actors as her band, 1984

Ivy wiping away a tear, taking a bow, at the end of *Silver Lady*'s opening night, 1984

Ivy receiving honorary degree from Leeds Polytechnic, with "old girl" Sheila Tracy, trombonist, 1987

Unveiling a memorial plaque on Ivy's childhood home, Cemetery Road Holbeck, Leeds, 2011

11

THE POSTWAR BAND

Her mother handed over a flimsy telegram envelope that had just arrived. Telegrams usually meant trouble. Sylvia England opened it with some trepidation, the arrival of such a telegram not being normal for a Huddersfield girl of fifteen. When she read the contents, an invitation from the famous bandleader Ivy Benson to join her, she jumped at the chance. Recently having left school, Sylvia had been destined, like many other girls in the Yorkshire wool town, to be a millworker. She had already agreed to start work in two days' time, and her overalls were ready. She hadn't been looking forward to it. Now here was what many girls in 1947 would have died for: An escape from the drab postwar, heavily rationed life of a mill girl to professional musicianship. A life of glamor, excitement, and travel. The choice was for Sylvia, as we would say now, a no-brainer. She spent her sixteenth birthday on a troop ship, traveling to entertain the forces in Europe.

The way Sylvia England joined Ivy Benson was not atypical. Starting in 1939 and during the many years that she led bands, Ivy provided opportunities for well over 250 women to have high-profile careers in music. The impact of Ivy on the lives of women as band instrumentalists cannot be underestimated. It was not until well into the 1950s that significant numbers of women began to sustain these careers independently, performing alongside men at the highest levels. Many women who were given their first break in the Benson band went on to become major British jazz artists. Sylvia had borrowed her brother's trumpet and, by age fifteen, had mastered the instrument and played well. She had played in a brass band and a youth orchestra in Huddersfield, but by age fifteen her music career seemed over. Mill life beckoned. But Ivy Benson, the bandleader whose all-women band had grown and prospered in the war years, was still, postwar, keeping an eagle eye open for up-and-coming female musicians and was prepared to train them into the professional players she needed to ensure her band's success in the coming years. Such a strategy was essential as the turnover of instrumentalists was always very high due to girls leaving, usually for marriage; Ivy rarely had the same lineup for more than six months at a time. Ivy knew that in Huddersfield lived a promising young trumpeter, Sylvia, almost old enough to travel with her band. And when the time came, Ivy sent for her.

Although many players were recruited from the North, where Ivy originated, the band was a route out of the conventional life of postwar Britain for many young women from all over the country. Women who had been used to freedom in the war, doing jobs that prewar had been the exclusive prerogative of men, suddenly saw things change. Women were praised for their wartime work but were expected to make way for the returning troops. Just as it had been after World War I, there was an assumption that their temporary roles had been specifically linked to wartime, and the government encouraged a return to domesticity. By 1951 the number of working women had returned almost to prewar levels but no higher, and a bar on married women working continued in many jobs. Women who found employment in the Civil Service, in teaching and in medicine, had to leave when they got married. And the trade unions still defended higher wages for men, despite an increase in women's union membership.

There were differences between areas of the country. Where women had traditionally worked in factories and mills, such as in Lancashire in the northwest of England, they continued to do so after the war, merely changing what they produced from war goods back to peacetime wares. In parts of the South where women had not traditionally worked, the men came back to take over jobs, and the women returned to domestic life, not unthankfully in many cases. It wasn't only the availability of interesting work after the war that affected both men's and women's perceptions of female roles and capabilities; many wanted society to return to what they had considered normal, with men in jobs and women as homemakers. People often spoke of life "before the war" or "in peacetime," looking backward or forward to a better life. Although people knew that postwar Britain could not be the same as it had been before, there was a nostalgia for it. Many women had lost husbands, fiancés, and boyfriends to war, and the men who did return sometimes seemed strangers, having experienced different relationships, places, and conditions not shared by the women. It is not surprising, then, that the thought of a warm, secure home with an attentive, well-dressed wife waiting for her husband to return from well-paid work, his slippers warming and a delicious meal prepared, had appeal for some of both sexes.

Most women did work when they left school, but for many it was still seen as an interval between education and marriage. In the early 1950s, over 60 percent of fifteen-year-old girls were in full-time work, but only just over 1 percent would go on to further education. There was a subtle, or maybe not-so-subtle, postwar intention to encourage women to think of themselves once again as homemakers primarily and to leave the interesting jobs to the men. Even the 1942 Beveridge Report on welfare, which aimed to improve the lives of everyone in postwar Britain, and indeed did so, implicitly assumed a role for women that today we would find unacceptable. But it merely reflected the prevailing attitude of the time. Beveridge wrote,

> The great majority of married women must be regarded as occupied on work which is vital though unpaid. Without which their husbands could not do their paid work and without which the nation could not continue. . . . The attitude of the housewife to gainful employment outside the home is not and should not be the same as that of a single woman. She has other duties. . . . In the next

thirty years housewives as Mothers have vital work to do in en-
suring the adequate continuance of the British Race and of British
ideals in the world.

Surprising, perhaps, to our modern ears, many women bought in to
this view of postwar life. Six years of bombs, shortages, and make-do-
and-mend years had left people drab and careworn. Women yearned
for a forgotten age of 1930s grace and femininity, even though this
had never been a reality for most of them. Women's magazines were
extremely popular in the postwar period: articles on clothes, cooking,
childcare, and decor dominated; there was hardly any coverage of
women at work. Virginia Nicholson, in her excellent book *Perfect
Wives in Ideal Homes*, about women in the 1950s, cites Monica Dickens
writing in *Woman's Own*: "Don't try to be the boss," writes Dickens.
"Marriage is the goal of every female who seeks happiness . . . It was
not intended by Nature that a woman should have to fend for herself."
Television, radio programs, and films of the early postwar period
also encouraged these attitudes. The new Queen Elizabeth, who came
to the throne in 1953, was used as an exemplar of the ideal woman.
Somehow the hardworking life of the modern monarch we know her
to be was conveniently overlooked in favor of seeing the queen as a
stay-at-home mother in a beautiful home with a handsome husband
and a young family. Refreshingly, her sister, Princess Margaret, never
fit into the mold, despite attempts by the establishment to control
her. The powers that be blocked her marriage to divorced Group
Captain Peter Townsend, and she eventually married photographer
and filmmaker Anthony Armstrong Jones, divorcing him in 1978,
which caused the princess much negative publicity. She was roman-
tically linked to several men and was often viewed as a controversial
member of the British royal family. Unlike her sister, Margaret was
certainly not considered a role model for the ideal of postwar womanhood that dominated at the time.
American and British films also supported the idea of wife and
mother as the acme of achievement for young women. As a small

child of the baby boom generation, the generation with no experience of wartime but whose parents were intimately involved with it, I remember going to see Doris Day in *Calamity Jane* three times. I thought her a splendid role model, and I practiced slapping my thigh and singing "The Deadwood Stage" in my bedroom. But this was the 1950s. Late in the film, even Calamity turned into a 1950s woman. Flourishing a feather duster to clean the cabin for her man, she sang "A Woman's Touch" as she did so.

> With a rub rub here and a rub rub there
> She can polish up the winders.

Although I probably could not have articulated the reason then, it was a great disappointment to my younger self!

Slowly, opportunities increased for women looking for greater professional choice, but it took a lot of determination and family backing to break away from the norm. The tripartite system of education, with the possibility of a grammar school education for the lucky girls who passed their eleven-plus examination, meant that careers rather than just jobs were available to some. But even women who did make it into previously male-dominated fields accepted inequalities and gender typecasting as the norm. "Even Diana Athill, Oxford educated and later to become a founding director of the publishing house André Deutsch, who at that time was single, entirely uninterested in food, and barely able to boil an egg, was given the Andre Deutsch cookery list to edit," comments Nicholson. Many women happily embraced a domestic role, but others chafed at the restrictions.

In the postwar austerity of the late 1940s and 1950s, a well-paid life of travel and glamor with its accompanying independence was very attractive to women musicians. Some, those who could play an instrument or sing but had few outlets for their talents, were happy to join bands like Ivy's as an interesting interlude between school and marriage. It was at least a change from the factory or office. There was the added bonus, too, of meeting many men from different backgrounds and therefore potentially having more choice of future partners than would have been available in their hometowns. This attitude caused many headaches for Ivy. She carefully trained musicians only to lose them to marriage. But for other women, some already playing professionally, it was a route to a long-lasting musical career. Whatever their motivation, for as long as Ivy's bands existed, aspiring female musicians from all over the country applied to her for an audition.

Eunice Cox from Bulwell, Nottingham, in the East Midlands, was typical. Born into a musical family, her mother, unusually for a woman in the 1930s, ran her own band in the Nottingham area. Her younger brother Colin ran a big band, playing the swing music of Glenn Miller and Benny Goodman. Eunice played violin and then took lessons in clarinet and saxophone from Jimmy Honeyman, a well-known bandleader in the East Midlands at that time. Eunice was determined to have a career as a professional musician, and having spent eighteen months with Gloria Gaye, she joined Ivy Benson's band. For instrumentalists such as Eunice, already playing professionally, there was no audition as such. She just turned up at a rehearsal and played along. She obviously played well. Ivy hired Eunice, and she spent a "wonderful" seven years touring at home and abroad with the band.

Singers too were recruited widely. Gloria Russell was one such. A talented young singer and impressionist, Gloria was saved by Ivy from life behind an Exeter department store jewelry counter. "There's a telegram for you, Gloria" announced her mother. "It's Ivy Benson, and she wants you to join her band." Gloria met up with Ivy and the other band members at Paddington Station. "Where are we going?" she asked. "Germany" was the answer. Gloria, who had never left Exeter, let alone Britain, was off with the band to play in the ruins of Berlin in the aftermath of war, followed by Austria and Italy. It was the start of her travels in a fantastic, well-paid job with Ivy that she enjoyed, on and off, for many years. Gloria sang with the band for ten years. She enjoyed life on the road, appearing with the band on the same bills as many young, soon-to-be stars. "Most became famous after I'd known them," she said in an interview in later life. "I kissed Eamonn Andrews, went to the pictures with Max Bygraves, saw a bit of Frankie Vaughan, and canoodled with a very funny young man in a double act—Eric Morecambe."

Ivy wanted the best, and when she heard a player she thought was right for her lineup, she was persistent in trying to engage her. Having initially tried but failed to persuade the young Gracie Cole to join her in the early 1940s, she kept in touch with her throughout the war. But it wasn't until late 1945 when Ivy's band returned from a tour abroad that Ivy got her wish. The trumpeter joined the band on November 2, 1945, at the age of twenty-one. "I'll always remember the date," said Gracie. "The first thing Ivy did when I joined the band was take me to Boosey and Hawkes, the most famous music shop in the world, and buy me a trumpet." And so began an unforgettable five years with Ivy.

But Ivy lost her instrumentalists sometimes because they were so good and other bands wanted them too. In April 1950, George Evans's band was playing in Grimsby, North Lincolnshire, with young Bill Geldard on trombone, having gotten leave from the air force to play with Evans. Ivy's band arrived in the same town to play for a week at the Palace Theatre, and Evans, seeing an opportunity for good publicity, arranged for the two bands to play together. They contacted the press and had a whole page in the *New Musical Express*. The men and women were interspersed, and the women trumpeters—Gracie, Sylvia England, and Dorothy Burgess—made a big impression. Bill Geldard reported that "some of the trumpet parts that had been missing [in the Evans band] were coming through loud and clear." He was given the job of approaching Gracie to ask her if she would like to join the Evans band, and despite the drop in pay, from eighteen guineas to ten pounds a week, she joined the band in August. Unfortunately for Ivy, who was not pleased at losing this fine trumpeter, romance too was involved in Gracie's decision. She married Bill the following February. But there were no hard feelings. When Gracie formed her own band some years later, she was appreciative of the advice and help from her former boss.

Other band members too were grateful for Ivy's keen eye for talent. In 1944 Henry Croudson, who years earlier had spotted Ivy and encouraged her to join his wife's band, was running a youth orchestra in Liverpool. Realizing that in the young Paula Pyke he had a girl who could be a professional musician, he encouraged his young drummer, already well known in her area, to apply to Ivy for an audition. He knew that she had real potential and that Ivy would give her a chance. In 1946, still only sixteen, Paula joined Ivy Benson and provided the beat behind the band for over sixteen years.

Another northern player was Margaret Chappell, from Sheffield, who played double bass with her brother's band, the Carmen Chappelle Accordion Band. With the band, Margaret played for nightly troop shows and weekend concerts with many professional performers. Later she joined her brother Walter's dance band, the resident band at the Cutlers' Hall, Sheffield. Both Gloria Gaye, the leader of Gloria Gaye's Ladies Band, and Ivy wanted Margaret to join their ensembles, but wartime regulations prevented Margaret's leaving her work. However, she played for Gloria during her vacation week and joined the Gloria Gaye Band at the end of the war. But Ivy still wanted her. In 1946, she approached Margaret again and obviously made her an offer she couldn't refuse. She joined Ivy's band and toured with them until 1948, when she married.

Although during the war and into the postwar period there were a number of all-female bands, some led by women, it was Gloria Gaye's band that would often compete with Ivy for the best instrumentalists. Born Marjorie Newman, Gaye led several all-female lineups as Gloria Gaye and Her Glamour Girls Band, which at various times was billed as Gloria Gaye and Her All Ladies Orchestra, Gloria Gaye All Girls Band, and Sweet Music and Hot Rhythm. Ivy did not always get her way. Sheelagh Pearson, born in 1928, grew up in Kent and was an accomplished accordionist but changed to drums at twenty. Arriving back from a Gibraltar night club job in 1952, she found two offers waiting for her, one from Ivy Benson and the other from trumpeter Gracie Cole, who had just formed her own orchestra. Sheelagh played a few times with both bands but then chose to join Gracie. Author and scholar of cultural studies George McKay, commenting on the reminiscences of Rene Ames, saw Gracie's band as demonstrating early signs of what he called "the shift from female to feminist activity." Ames said, "Gracie's band was that little bit better than Ivy's only because Gracie believed that she wanted us to look like men and play like men but Ivy was more into showmanship, more of a cabaret and more of what people wanted to see. Gracie always had us dressing in suits, straight skirts below the knee, and men's jackets. Ivy's was more feminine than Gracie's ever was."

So even as early as the 1950s, things were changing. Women in the newer bands were beginning to reject the need to look "feminine" as well as play well. And it was Gracie's band, not Ivy's, that was the first all-girl band to perform at London's Jazz Jamboree at the Gaumont State Cinema in Kilburn. In 1956, Sheelagh Pearson joined the Lena Kidd Quartet. Lena, a tenor saxophonist, had played in both Ivy's and Gloria Gaye's bands.

Ivy did not expect all the girls to be expert players when she hired them; she spotted potential and was prepared to develop it. She often had no choice. As she said, "If, say, Ted Heath lost a trumpet player he would call trumpeters in other bands and get a replacement. I had to start again and make one." Known as a great enabler, she once said proudly, "I took a girl from a pie factory once and made her a bass guitarist."

Sylvia England remembered Ivy as a great teacher. "Her determination, persistence, dedication, and knowledge were legendary. When I had to take over lead trumpet, it was the most terrifying experience of my musical career. But when Ivy made up her mind that one of us had to do something for her, we most certainly had to get on with it and do it. By sheer determination and willpower she would work with us until we were as good as she wanted us to be." On one tour in 1950, Sylvia mentioned to Ivy that she had a sister Dorothy who had just started playing the trombone. Ivy decided that she could soon teach Dorothy all she needed to know, so the younger girl joined her sister in the band, and Ivy "spent hours teaching her bass clef, the dance band idiom, section playing, and so on." Dorothy stayed with Ivy for six years and became lead trombone, even receiving praise and a signed photograph from Tommy Dorsey—"From one good trombonist to another."

Although Ivy nurtured talent, she had to learn when to let go gracefully, says Lucy O'Brien in her book *She Bop*. In a letter to Gracie Cole when the trumpeter decided to form her own band, Ivy advised, "One of the first things to remember is certain instruments consider themselves hard to replace and one is tempted to do anything to keep them, even spend sleepless nights. Do not let it happen to you . . . remember the only important person in the outfit is yourself and you call the tune . . . Don't make the mistakes I did, love."

As the immediate postwar years ended and there were more women learning instruments both as amateurs and with formal music education, the pool of potential band members increased. There was still a high turnover, but Ivy carried extra brass players, at least four trumpeters, and four trombonists instead of three, especially when gigging at US bases—"just in case." In the late 1950s, the Benson band was well known and seen by many as a route to a career, and Ivy never lacked for applications.

By the 1950s, there were more women in bands and groups all over the country. There was more flexibility too from this time, as confident women moved in and out of groups as opportunities presented themselves. Life with Ivy was no longer seen by most as the gap between school and marriage but as a way of getting more experience and as a route to a fulfilling life in music.

In 1954, Ivy needed a female double bass player to replace one who was leaving. She found out that in Bradford there was a sixteen-year-old girl, Claudia Colmer, who was a cello player but whose father had taught her to play the double bass alongside him. Claudia's mother, who mistakenly had the idea that a ladies' orchestra was a sedate band that played in cafés and hotels, took her daughter to London for an audition that was held in Ivy's apartment in the

Cumberland Hotel near Marble Arch. Claudia was accepted. She didn't return home but instead went straight to the seaside to begin her professional career. Ivy instructed Claudia's mother to go back to Bradford and send Mr. Colmer's double bass down to Torquay, where the band was booked for the summer season. The instrument was duly sent by train to Torquay in the guard's van, and Claudia's father, bereft of his double bass, had to go out and buy a replacement. Ivy paid for Claudia to have bass lessons, and after practice in the summer with the orchestra, the sixteen-year-old became a full member of Ivy's big band. She stayed for eight years, from 1954 to 1962.

Sheila Tracy joined Ivy as a trombonist in 1956 direct from her studies at the Royal Academy of Music, where she had studied piano, violin, and trombone. Sheila had been wondering what she would do to earn a living after her studies when someone suggested she write to Ivy Benson. She was invited to meet Ivy and the girls at a Lyons Corner House where the band was playing. Sheila thought the band was so glamorous in their orange strapless dresses. Despite not having a clue how to play the theme from *Riffifi* that Ivy had put in front of her, she was hired and joined Ivy at the Ideal Home Show in Edinburgh at the end of the spring term. Sheila remembered that her father was delighted to be saved a term's student fees for the Royal Academy. At that time the amount of prejudice against women was stifling, she said; women were criticized and considered pretty but not able to play the same way as a man. After two years, Sheila left Ivy feeling confident enough to form a comedy music duo, the Tracy Sisters, with fellow trombonist and singer Phyll Brown. Sheila later became a well-known broadcaster. Hosting Big Band Special on BBC Radio 2 from the 1970s for twenty-one years, she enjoyed standing in on trombone or as conductor on occasions. Like many of Ivy's "old girls," Sheila stayed in touch and remained a friend.

June Pressley was a beautician in Fraserburgh in the northeast of Scotland when, in 1956, she applied to Ivy for a job. She played the piano mostly but also the alto saxophone in her father's band. He had encouraged her to apply to Ivy and took her to the Isle of Man for her audition. Coincidentally, that Sunday a photograph of June in a bikini was on the front page of the *News of the World*. A photographer had seen her in Fraserburgh and asked her to pose for him. June thought that it helped her to get the job, as Ivy had run up to Johnny Dankworth and Cleo Laine, also playing at the Villa Marina that week, waving the newspaper, saying "Look at my new sax player."

Despite not being the tenor sax player that Ivy needed, June was hired. She went home and immediately bought a tenor sax for fourteen pounds from her cousin, and Ivy taught her to play it. June was delighted with her new job. The first wage she received from Ivy was twelve pounds, and though she had to pay her own rent and some other expenses, June was happy; it was a great improvement on the two pounds she had received working at the beauty salon. Like all the women in the band, June became used to working alongside many stars of the period. Singer Frankie Vaughan was very handsome, and girls were always hanging around his dressing room. One day June wrote to her father to say she had just seen him in a string vest, fashionable at the time. Her father retorted "You'll never play like Coleman Hawkins if you're going to look at Frankie Vaughan in his string vest."

Always with a chair to fill, Ivy kept a lookout for suitable future band members when she shared the bill with other groups. In the summer of 1953 for example, Ivy's band was playing alongside Jack Leon's orchestra on the Isle of Man. Leon was well known in the 1940s and 1950s, appearing regularly on *Music While You Work*, an iconic program of the war years. At the end of the season, Ivy recruited Jean Curphey, a local singer who had performed with Leon, to join her own twenty-four-piece band for a winter season at the Quebec Restaurant at Marble Arch.

But perhaps the nicest recruitment story is that of Eva Clarke. A lively redhead who worked at the Singer Sewing Machine factory in Glasgow, Eva and some friends were on holiday on the Isle of Man in the summer of 1965 when they ran out of pocket money. Eva decided to enter the local talent contest, as there was a cash prize. One of the judges was Ivy. Eva chose to sing "The Wedding," a song then in the charts sung by Julie Rogers. Ivy said, "I seldom heard such quality in a voice." She booked Eva to sing with the band on afternoons for the rest of the week before she went back to Glasgow and invited her back to the island a fortnight later to sing with her for the rest of the season. Whether Eva continued her new career or went back to her factory job is unclear, but at least the pocket-money problem was solved.

12

ON THE ROAD

Berlin was just the start of many visits made by Ivy and her band to British and American bases in Belgium, Holland, and Germany and of more extensive tours all over Europe. Their first tour of Germany was in 1946, a highlight of which was a concert with singer and wartime French Resistance agent Josephine Baker. Then Ivy took the band on an ENSA tour, followed by a trip to Ostend to play for some special occasion at which Maurice Chevalier presented a grand prize, and a couple of months later they were booked at the Tivoli Gardens in Stockholm.

From 1947 and well into the 1960s, the band continued to tour abroad extensively entertaining troops, interspersed with other bookings and summer seasons by the British seaside. In the late 1940s, the Ivy Benson band was booked to play summer seasons at Butlin's seaside holiday camps in the towns of Filey in Yorkshire, and Skegness in Lincolnshire. Billy Butlin's policy was to provide the best of British entertainment and include it in the price of package holidays. Later, the Isle of Man (eighteen summers at the Villa Marina), and Jersey, among many others, were regular seaside destinations for Ivy. Staff at all the major ports, airports, and railway stations got to know her and were ready to help get the band members, the instruments, and luggage aboard their transport as quickly as possible.

Although male bandleaders were increasingly returning from the war and taking up their batons again, Ivy could attract large loyal audiences among those who had listened to and enjoyed her wartime broadcasts. She was recognized at home now, and her celebrity status was confirmed when the band played at the 1948 Summer Olympic Games in London, a rare honor. By 1949, Ivy was also in demand further afield, playing in the Middle East at military bases in Egypt, Malta, Cyprus, and Tripoli.

Music critic Tony Parker, writing in 2004, recalled the first time he saw Ivy's band, in 1956. He wrote that it was not one of the best bands he'd ever heard, although he felt that the same was true for many male bands. But he remembered the glamor element of her players and her style; this appealed to audiences, and that was all that really mattered. She played the kind of neat, precise music "beloved of the up-tempo brigade," and the fact that she had come to fame in wartime made her band the ideal choice to entertain troops stationed overseas for many years after the war had ended. Parker's estimate of the quality of Ivy's band music seems a little unfair. Many of the women who played in Ivy's band were consummate jazz musicians, and if the audience's taste warranted it, could produce sophisticated jazz numbers. In their heyday of the late 1950s, they were often on television and at the Palladium, and the name Ivy Benson was referenced alongside names such as Geraldo or Jack Payne, both still popular bandleaders at that time.

Ivy and her players' life on the road, playing for the troops, made for a lot of good stories. Once, after a tour in Austria, the band was on its way to Trieste when Ivy came across three young children—two brothers and their sister, who was only eight and crying. Part of a Hungarian circus act trying to get back to Hungary, the youngsters had been stranded on the wrong side of the border. Their parents had not had the right papers to get them out of Austria, and the couple had made a run for it into Italy, hoping the children would follow. But without papers and so unable to get visas, the three children couldn't cross the border. Ivy made a risky decision: She and her wardrobe mistress wrapped up the children as warmly as they could and hid them under a portable rostrum in the back of the luggage van and moved racks of clothes in front of it. Ivy told Gloria Russell, her vocalist on the tour, to sit with the driver and distract the guards at the border post. At the customs hut, Ivy told the girls to get out and take some of the booze they had been given on tour and entertain the border personnel. Meanwhile, Gloria chatted animatedly with the guards inspecting the interior of the lorry, telling them she was a singer with the band, and before they got past the first rack of dresses, they'd lost interest in the job. After a half-hearted search, they allowed the lorry through the checkpoint. At Trieste, the girls put the children on the train with a collection of Italian money that they had made. Ivy never heard from them again.

Each year throughout the 1950s, and for many years afterward, Ivy would take her band to Germany to play for the American troops stationed there. A regular tour was to the Ramstein Air Base near Kaiserslautern. There they played mostly for the noncommissioned officers but occasionally for the higher ranks, too. Claudia Lang-Colmer remembers that all the band members had officer status and were issued PX cards, which allowed them to purchase things from the stores on the base; goods such as chocolate milk and Old Spice aftershave, which was intended for men but used as perfume by the women. All the goods were shipped in from the United States, and although rationing in Britain had ended in 1954, the range of things that could be bought in the American stores must have seemed amazing to English visitors. The regular visits to Ramstein were very enjoyable, but Claudia does recall a poignant, sad note: On a raised dais in the middle of the camp stood a mangled wreck of a car, the "crash of the month." Although American beer was freely available, the young airmen preferred the much stronger German variety. The Autobahn had no speed limit, and many crashes killed or maimed young men serving in Germany. The displayed wreck was an attempt to warn against the consequences of excess drinking and excess speed.

Working in the Middle East too made for many enjoyable and sometimes funny moments. On one tour in Egypt, the band was traveling across miles of desert toward a base where they were to perform. The truck with the instruments had gone ahead. One of the girls, looking out of the window, turned to Ivy. "I know there are mirages out here, but tell me if I'm looking at a bass drum in the middle of the desert." They had to stop and collect their drum, which had fallen off the instrument truck. In the desert too, Ivy recalled that once in 1971, the band members noticed that costumes kept disappearing from a basket on board their bus. Then they discovered that a hole had been made in the roof and that a group of locals had been hooking the costumes out. "There must be a band of Arabs walking 'round the desert in pink nylon dresses," Ivy speculated wryly.

Conditions on tour could be primitive. On the way from one army base to another, the band stopped at an old army building in the desert where the lavatories were just holes in the ground in little cubicles. Suddenly, Ivy let out a piercing scream, and when the girls rushed in to the outhouse, wondering what was wrong, she was pointing down the hole saying, "There's an animal down there." They all stared down the hole where they saw a drenched desert rat, looking up at them.

The band played in makeshift theaters, usually tin huts. One night the plan had been for the band to enter in the dark onto the stage. There would be a fanfare, the lights would go up on the glamorous band, and Ivy would start the music. That night, the signal was given, the trumpets blared, but then pandemonium broke loose. Bats came swooping out of the rafters, the girls screamed, and the troops rolled about with laughter. At another concert, a troop of large humpback ants proceeded to march out of the back of the piano, an ancient upright. That night the girls played standing on chairs. But it was a great evening, and there was a party after the show. At one base the impromptu dressing room was on stilts, and four armed guards were posted outside. With twenty minutes to go before the show, the players began to change into stage costumes and do their makeup. Gloria Russell, whom Ivy remembered as "very well-endowed," stripped to get ready. Suddenly she yelled, and Ivy rushed to see what was happening. A row of eyes along the cracks in the floor boards was peering up. Ivy wasn't having that; she called the military police.

But even if the theaters were makeshift, the gigs were well organized. When the band was based at Ismailia, about eighty miles northeast of Cairo, Ivy was routinely informed exactly when the coach was to be at the base and that the instruments would be loaded on a truck to go on before them, to meet them at their destination. And usually they were. After the show, the band would return to base to await traveling instructions for the next destination.

Being responsible for an ever-changing group of young women, some still in their teens, was one of Ivy's trials. Because of the constant need to replenish the band lineup, Ivy often employed very young women—fifteen-, sixteen-, and seventeen-year-olds—whom she was prepared to train up to her professional music standards. To take them out of the United Kingdom, she had to register them with the police—at Scotland Yard for those living in London and at Bow Street for the others. Parents had to give their permission for Ivy to be responsible for their daughters. Once the band was abroad, Ivy had to declare the girls at the consulate in each town they visited. When Paula Pyke joined Ivy, she was one of six underage band members. She remembered being asked questions like "was she getting enough food?" and "was everything alright?" Everything was certainly alright; these young girls, with little life experience, fresh out of Britain and independent for the first time, were having a ball. They needed firm handling. Dressed just like the older women in the band, they looked more mature than they were. On many tours, the girls were entertaining all-male audiences, clamoring for them, and all Ivy's skills as a chaperone, protector, and boss were needed.

Ivy was insistent on good behavior from her band. One of her postwar instrumentalists, comparing her own life touring with Ivy and that of musicians of a later generation, commented, "Ivy didn't like you to act flirty—didn't mind a little flirt but not to cheapen yourself. It wouldn't have been good for the band. Ours was a different era; the girls now are much more blatant about sex and talk about it. Of course, we didn't have the pill, did we? We were too scared. If I got into trouble, my father would have killed me."

In later years, Ivy spoke of her surprise that she hadn't had too many problems of delinquency and that in all her years in the business had never had any complaints from parents or from any consulate. Of course, there were things she *did* have to deal with. On one occasion, she advertised for a trombone player, and a promising young girl of only fifteen applied. As usual, Ivy applied to Scotland Yard for the usual police license, and a doctor pronounced the girl fit and able to travel. The young new recruit flew out to join the band on tour. After a couple of weeks, Ivy noticed the girl had put on weight and suggested that she watch her food intake, as there was only one set of stage clothes. One of the older women took Ivy aside and quietly told her that the girl was pregnant and had been when she'd come from England. Ivy rang Scotland Yard to say that the girl was being sent back, and in the same state that she had come out. Ivy found out later that the girl had been going out with a soldier stationed in London and that her mother had wanted her out of his way. Whether the mother knew of the girl's pregnancy is not known.

Ivy was equally tough if she thought her authority was being undermined. She was very accommodating to the requests of the troops for whom her band played; there were no ENSA guidelines, and Ivy had free rein. The band had played many sentimental songs in wartime as well as swing, but now their repertoire expanded to include popular songs and novelty numbers. But this did not suit all the girls. One of Ivy's best musicians got drunk one night and tore up her music, saying that she wasn't prepared to play German drinking songs; they weren't proper music. Ivy fired her on the spot. She couldn't accept such behavior in front of the young ones. However, there were no hard feelings, and the woman kept in touch with Ivy, even apologizing for her conduct years later.

Ivy was a professional through and through and insisted that her band play to the highest standards. There were no excuses for poor performance. Gloria Russell, who had never been out of Exeter before joining Ivy's band, found herself onstage at the Hamburg opera house on her first night, in 1947. Jack McVea's then-popular novelty number "Open the Door, Richard" had just been added to the repertoire, and Gloria, as vocalist, had to sing the title line. Timing was all. Gloria missed the beat, turned her back on the audience, and ran back to her seat. Ivy carried on conducting the band and smiled at the audience over her shoulder. As she turned around, she glared at her vocalist: "Don't you ever do that again," she said. And then the smile was back on.

Although she always insisted that the band was a business and not a family—how could it be, with a large, ever-changing group of girls?—Ivy had to play the role of mother—or at least big sister—at times. On tour, she insisted that the underage girls stay in the hotel at night with her. She was freer with the older ones. According to Gloria, who stayed with the band for ten years and practically grew up with Ivy, she never queried what they did, instead assuming an attitude of, "It's your life; you go out and do what you want to, but be careful, and watch what you're doing." But Ivy always checked that they were all back in the hotel safely, so unless they were to keep her up through the night and incur her wrath, they knew that very late nights weren't a good idea. But girls will be girls, and her band members often found ways to outwit her. Gillian Dennis, who played alto sax with Ivy in the late 1950s, recalled that one night some of the band had met up with the boys from the Eric Delaney band who had invited the girls out to a nightclub. "'Oh no—Ivy would be absolutely furious if we did that,' we said. 'Well,'" they replied, "'try and sneak out.'" And sneak out they did. They couldn't go out the door without being, seen so they knotted sheets together and threw them out the window. They left one volunteer behind who pulled up the makeshift rope and then flushed the toilet at intervals so Ivy wouldn't suspect they were out.

And of course there were the GIs. An average of 27 percent of all US troops were stationed abroad in the 1950s, mostly in East Asia and Europe but also the Middle East. When Ivy's band visited those American bases, there were more than enough young men to cause problems for her. Although her girls attracted British servicemen, of all the headaches that Ivy had to contend with, losing instrumentalists to American servicemen was the worst, and she regularly had to read-vertise back in Britain for replacements to fly out to join her tours. The girls were in the public eye and appeared fresh and smart to the lonely young men, often based in the middle of desert areas where there were no women at all. Sometimes the young men would propose after a mere twenty-four hours' acquaintance. Some of these rapid romances worked out: these postwar brides from the band found themselves sailing to new lives in the United States, many to live happily ever after but occasionally to face disillusion. And there were the sad ones who succumbed to the "fast-talking Texans whose ranches and oil-fields turned out to exist only in lines learned from the Hank Janson/Mickey Spillane school of Romeos," which became an oft-told joke. Ivy remembered one girl with stars in her eyes over the GI she was going to marry who turned out to have a wife and two children back in Mississippi.

One would think that the comparative attractions of GIs would have ended as the 1950s progressed, people became more affluent, and rationing ended. But no—even in the late 1960s, when an American serviceman could no longer buy his fun with chocolate and nylons, for Ivy's girls he still beat every other uniform in sight. "They are very fast workers," Ivy observed wryly, speaking in March 1968, proceeding to tick off on her fingers the names of band members she'd lost to marriage with GIs: "Five marriages last year, and so far this year, it's two marriages and two engagements."

But despite all the ups and downs of life on tour, Ivy never re-gretted all the years she spent playing to servicemen and -women. Things changed slowly but inevitably, and by the late 1950s the band was playing mostly mainstream venues and summer seasons with fewer military bookings. But neither joys nor the travails of touring a band stopped. Anne Blair, who played with the band in 1957 and 1958, reminisced in 1984 about those tours. In the summer she found herself playing every afternoon in the Villa Marina gardens on the Isle of Man, in all weathers. Single-night engagements were mostly in the winter. It was cold, especially sitting in an unheated coach for up to twelve hours as the band traveled between gigs. Sheepskin-coated and wearing two of everything, hair in rollers under tea-cozy hats, they headed north up the A5. Ivy wore her mink. To Anne, a young twenty-year-old, the experience was quite heady, and she'd begun to think that she and the band were something special. That was until they were booked for one night in a small town in Lancashire. "As the coach bumped across the level crossing, gateway to this northern mill town, I said to Jean Smith, the Brummie tenor sax player, 'This will be a pushover.'" How wrong they were. While getting ready in the ladies' cloakroom, they heard the "big, fat sound" of a first-rate dance band, and, looking over the balcony, they saw a mere fourteen-piece band making the rich, full sound. "Of course," Anne said, "we were in brass band country." They were listening to a band that had recently won the Melody Maker award for the best semiprofessional band in the country. So why had they bothered booking Ivy's band? The answer was, she said, that Ivy Benson's band at the time was a name band and that audiences wanted to see and hear her.

In an interview later in her life, Ivy was asked if she remembered one particular cold, wintry night in 1957 when she and her band had been booked to appear at the Pavilion Gardens in Buxton. The town had been virtually cut off by snow, and the band was stranded fifteen miles away. The players had to change into their stage costumes in the coach. They'd eventually made it at 10 p.m., two hours late. Ivy *did* remember.

"I remember that night very well," she laughed. "In fact, it was one of the coldest that I have ever spent. Have you ever tried playing a sax suffering from near frostbite?"

13

IVY THE WOMAN

It is difficult to know Ivy the person as distinct from Ivy Benson the bandleader and show-business personality, her personal life was so integrated with that of her work. Much of the working year, and for most of any year she *was* working, Ivy spent away from home, traveling at the head of her troop of young women. It is almost inevitable, then, that most of her friends were in the entertainment business in some capacity, and similarly peripatetic. Within that business, however, she had become well liked and knew everyone. The list of people alongside whom she played on tours, in concert halls, and in summer seasons, many of whom she considered friends, reads like a roll call of who's who in the popular entertainment world of the 1950s, 1960s, and 1970s: Jack Parnell, John Dankworth, Ken Mackintosh, Harry Secombe, Billy Cotton, and Edmundo Ross, to name just a few. Even Billy Ternent, who had once opposed her vehemently back in her early days as bandleader, had succumbed to her talent and professionalism, becoming a friend and supporter. During the years that she was running her band, Ivy worked alongside not only famous names but also those who would later become famous. Comedians Morecambe and Wise, who in later years became one of the best-known comedy partnerships in Britain, were just one of the supporting acts when Ivy topped the bill. They affectionately referred to her as Ivy Bunsen and Her Bunsen Burners when they had a show of their own a decade later.

For all her travel, Ivy remained very close to her parents, Digger and Mary. They had lost two sons—one in early childhood when Ivy was a newborn and one through illness at eighteen, a boy whom Digger had, like Ivy, taught music and for whom he'd cherished hopes of professional musicianship. Ivy had been the only daughter in the Benson family and by the time the war broke out the only child. She felt a great deal of responsibility for her parents and shared her success with them. It was, after all, her father who had taught her to play the piano, nurtured her early talent, and made her into the confident musician she was. By the 1940s, Ivy was employing her father as road manager, and he was well respected and liked in the business. Later in that decade, she was based in London at 20 New Cavendish Street, W1, and it was probably at this time that her parents moved south to live with her and look after the house during her extended tours. From 1948, when she'd begun spending summers playing for holiday-makers at coastal resorts, her parents would accompany her.

She looked after her father into his old age after her mother's death. In December 1976, Ivy was the subject of the popular television program *This Is Your Life*. Some of Ivy's past band members were flown in for the program, and host Eamonn Andrews talked to Ivy about her work as bandleader and her personal life, including where she had lived and her love of furs and jewelry. She was wearing a large ruby ring that night on the show. Toward the end of the taping, the old band members were asked to group around her in place of family members. The show made obvious, says Claudia Lang-Colmer, that she was wealthy and had an ailing father. Any viewer of that night's episode would also have been aware of the area where she lived: Unfortunately, the price of such fame was that in early 1977, not long after the episode aired, Ivy's home in Chiswick was broken into and robbed by two criminals. Her address had been in the phone book! The thieves took thousands of pounds' worth of jewelry and a mink coat worth three thousand pounds. Ivy had been out of the house at the time, playing at a British Legion club, but her father had been at home. The men beat up the eighty-six-year-old Digger, hitting him with a piece of metal tubing and tying him up. He died shortly afterward at Great Yarmouth, most likely as a result of his injuries. The two thieves went to prison for three years.

Ivy's success and renown took a toll on all aspects of her personal life, it seems. Her early years in the music business left little time for lasting romance, except as an onlooker to the relationships of her musicians. But by the late 1940s, perhaps when she was well-established and could make her own schedule, she found time for a serious love affair. Playing at Butlin's holiday camp at Filey in Yorkshire, she met Caryll Stafford Clark, a theatrical producer, and on October 19, 1949, they were married at Caxton Hall's register office in Westminster, the venue choice of many celebrities of that time. Her father served as one of her witnesses.

Caryll was the son of a well-known, real-life husband-and-wife team—Billy Caryll and Hilda Mundy—who in the 1930s had played on stage, radio, and on records as a bickering couple in *Scenes of Domestic Bliss*, although in real life they were known to be very close. One of their main claims to fame was having been original members of what would come to be known as the Crazy Gang. In 1931 three double acts—Nervo and Knox, Naughton and Gold, and Billy Caryll and Hilda Mundy—had been tentatively booked at the London Palladium by theater impresario George Black. Upon consideration, three acts had seemed too many, so he considered cancelling one of the couples. But Nervo and Knox had a technique of entering other acts as part of their comedy, and Black had been persuaded to let the original booking play out as it would. The show, which was called *Crazy Week*, opened on November 30 and became an instant success, and when Flanagan and Allen joined, just before Carryll and Mundy moved on to other things, the troupe had become popularly known as the Crazy Gang, although the name was not officially used until 1937. Carryll and Mundy continued their partnership and starred alongside George Formby in his 1945 film, *I Didn't Do It*.

In 1949, when Ivy married Clark Carryll Stafford, his "condition" on the wedding certificate was given as a widower and his age thirty-two. As a first marriage at thirty-five for the independent Ivy, and to a younger man who had been married before and lost his wife, the prospects weren't good. The new husband entertained another woman in Ivy's flat while she was away on tour. The marriage was short-lived, and the couple divorced a mere two years later.

Small, dark-haired, just over five feet in height, and slim, Ivy dressed elegantly, and not only for the stage. At the end of her playing career, she could fit into the same size of dress as at the start. She was very aware of the fact that she was Ivy Benson and would be recognized even when offstage. Off-duty photographs of the time often show her smartly dressed and in furs, not considered appropriate these days but part of the wardrobe of a well-dressed woman in the 1950s. More than twenty years later when her flat was burgled, those furs, including a mink coat—though likely no longer worn—formed part of the intruder's haul. In addition to wearing elegant furs, collecting jewelry was one of her passions, and she was known for wearing it. Sylvia England remembers sitting next to Ivy on the plane back from entertaining the troops in the Suez Canal zone in 1950, seeing Ivy use gin to clean her diamond rings. Ivy enjoyed gambling on slot machines, which were easily found in the summer-season locations where the band played. On occasion, she liked the glamor of casinos and usually found someone to take her bets to the bookies for big horse races.

All who worked with Ivy commented on how strict she was but also how this meant she was a respected leader. Sheila Tracy remembered being put on lead trombone one night, a change of instrument. All went well until the last number at one in the morning, when Ivy brought out an arrangement of "Rose Marie." Tracy cracked the top C. Ivy came down on her "like a ton of bricks." Ivy was particularly hard on the sax section because she herself was a saxophonist. Claudia Lang-Colmer played the double bass and was mainly left alone.

Although very bossy, Ivy was also sociable and fun. Happy to join in parties after shows, she liked a drink and was keen to seek out jazz clubs in cities where the band played. She often relaxed by playing there with local fellow musicians—a "mingle," as she called it. She was considered a celebrity by the public, and she enjoyed her fame. When the band was in one place for a season, she was happy when not performing to contribute her time to local activities. On the Isle of Man, she ran children's and teenage talent contests. In the late 1950s, the young Cyril Mead and Edward McGinis were given their first taste of fame in one such competition. They always remembered this, and years later, in 1976, by then established comedians Syd Little and Eddie Large, the duo invited her to appear on their pilot show for Thames Television. Ivy also judged beauty competitions, drew raffles, and handed out prizes. In 1957 she was even asked to give racing tips by the local racing paper. She tipped Rum Fun in the 3 o'clock at Bath one day in June 1957. The horse lost.

Comfortable on stage, Ivy was prepared to laugh with the audience if something untoward happened, unless it appeared to reflect on the quality of her music. Margaret Roe, who stood at a diminutive five-foot, one-half-inch tall, had to stand on a stool to play her double bass. One night she fell off it, tipping over the side of the stage, still clutching her bass. Ivy laughed so hard that she nearly brought the show to a standstill. June Pressley, who played tenor sax with Ivy for two years, said that she did have favorites, not as individuals but as instrumentalists. June remembered arriving at one venue to find that there were only photographs of the brass section on the wall outside— no saxes at all. "I'll never forget that," June said. But other brass players don't seem to have made similar comments, so perhaps the seeming favoritism was because trumpet players in a band are somewhat isolated from the rest of the ensemble. Exposed, they stand out when playing. At that time, the brass section may have needed Ivy's attention and coaching more than others in the band.

Ivy's work was her life, and for most of her life she was never out of work, having no holidays but just the odd day off between gigs. This did not leave much time to develop close friendships. Ivy's relationship with most of the girls had to be intimate in some ways, as the band members lived as well as worked together on tour and often shared dressing rooms. But essentially, she was their employer. She was always the one in authority, and perhaps benign dictatorship best describes her style of leading. She was tough and did not want to be loved or even liked as much as respected. It must have been a lonely life at times—particularly when on tour she had to keep a distance between herself and the band members to maintain discipline. The rest of the band had each other, and whatever the relationships between them, good or bad, there were always allies. Without a home and family to return to after work and what with all the pressures of organization and performance on her shoulders, Ivy must have felt alone even in the middle of such a large group of women. But ever the professional, she rarely confided her inner feelings to others.

Ivy had an enviable energy and capacity for work, but she did not always enjoy good health. She underwent five major operations over the years, including the removal of one of her kidneys, which prevented her from traveling to the Far East. Somehow she managed to fit operations and recuperation periods into her packed schedule like the well-organized businesswoman she was. As a result of her illness, she was unable to have children. Whether this was a problem for her is not clear, as she loved her traveling life and it seems doubtful that she ever would have given it up for domesticity. But it may have been an issue contributing to the difficulty of maintaining her marriages.

Many of her players came, stayed a year or two, and then left, but with just a few of the girls, particularly those who stayed with her for a long period, Ivy developed closer friendships. Paula Pyke was her drummer for fifteen years. Ivy had mothered Paula when she'd first joined as a teenager in 1947, and Paula grew up with the band. As time went on, Ivy would confide in her, and the younger woman was the first to know about Ivy's second marriage. As did many of her girls before and after, this time Ivy married an American serviceman.

Ivy met Top Sergeant Berthold Brantley Callaway of the US Air Force in 1955. Originally from Inglewood, California, and from a military family—his father was a retired colonel of the US Army—Brantley, as he was known, was a war veteran who had fought in Italy and Africa and served in Korea. As the entertainment manager at his Air Force base at Upper Heyford outside Oxford, he was responsible for booking acts to entertain the troops. He and Ivy met when he went down to scout her band, which was appearing at the Chiswick Empire in London. It seems to have been love at first sight, as he and Ivy were unofficially engaged only a week later. However, due to the unrelenting schedule of Ivy's work, two years had passed before they got around to marriage. It was hard for them to find time to see each other, but in 1957 they managed to reconnect on the Isle of Man, where Ivy and her band had visited each summer season for the last three years and would do so for another fifteen. That June, Brant joined her for a short holiday on the island, and they announced their coming marriage to the press. They couldn't give a date they said; they were waiting for the permission documents from US Army authorities. These duly arrived, and the wedding was planned for the end of the season, September 6, 1957.

It was a grand showbiz wedding. Two hundred guests, mostly from the world of entertainment, converged on the island. Only a small number of them—all twenty-three members of the band and a few close friends—attended the ceremony at 10 a.m. in the Douglas Civil Registry Office. Ivy was given away by her father, and Paula Pyke and Eddie W. Jones, a London impresario and good friend, served as witnesses. The bride wore a hyacinth-blue lace suit with a stand-away collar and a blue feathered hat. Paula was in a natural flecked suit trimmed with black velvet and a yellow feathered hat. A photograph of the newlywed couple signing the register shows Brant in civilian clothes and a buttonhole, with his left arm round his smiling bride; his right holds Ivy's white poodle, Peppi. The dog wore a special jeweled collar for the occasion. Brant was a lovely man, reports Claudia Lang-Colmer—very patient and kind. He was often, uncomplainingly, left to look after Ivy's spoiled dogs while she performed.

The wedding was followed by a big reception at the Villa Marina, and despite the rain, Ivy's band formed a guard of honor outside the reception venue with their instruments. Tiny musical instruments too decorated the three-tiered wedding cake. The list of those attending, and indeed those who couldn't attend but sent congratulations, shows the extent of Ivy's friendship circle. It included fellow entertainers, bandleaders Ken Mackintosh and Alyn Ainsworth, singer Frances Tanner of the Tanner Sisters, comedian Billy Stutt, editor of the influential *Melody Maker* magazine, Pat Brand, and Syd Plummer from the entertainment fraternity the Grand Order of Water Rats. There were scores of telegrams—among them from comedian Harry Secombe, advice columnist Marjorie Proops, writer-producer Richard Afton, bandleaders Billy Cotton and Edmundo Ross, and her erstwhile opponent Billy Ternent. And from the Crazy Gang, "Much happiness and congratulations. Do nothing till you hear from us."

The affection that the couple had for the Isle of Man and the island's people was obvious. There were presents from island groups, including a rug from the Old Time Dancing Circle. Brant showed his appreciation in a warm welcome speech: "To use a real American expression, I think you guys are swell." One-and-a-half hours after the reception, Ivy Benson Calloway was back at work, conducting her band at an afternoon concert at the Villa Marina.

It might have been around this time that Ivy decided to take five years off her age. In September 1957, she was just short of her forty-fourth birthday but gave her age for the marriage certificate as thirty-seven. Perhaps she wanted to appear younger to her groom, who was forty-three. It's unclear why she thought the deception necessary. She certainly could get away with the deduction—she was attractive, slim, and youthful—but it seems an odd thing for the successful, confident Ivy to do. She kept up the pretense for many years: in the 1980s, the *Guardian* newspaper featured her in its list of notable birthdays every November 11, and in 1984 she was, according to the paper, sixty-six (actually seventy-one) and in 1987, sixty-nine.

Unfortunately, her marriage to Calloway, like her first marriage, did not last. Unlike men, women often gave up their careers in music upon marriage, but that was not for Ivy. She continued her busy touring life, and Brant, who could have left the Army earlier, signed on for another six-year tour of duty almost immediately. In June 1960, the *Isle of Man Times* reported that Brant was visiting his wife on the island, where she was spending her usual summer season. He had ten days' leave. The couple had only seen each other for a few days over the last two years, as after the marriage he had served in the United Kingdom and Germany before being posted back to the United States in 1958. He had arrived back in Britain in May 1960, only two days before Ivy left for a month in Hamburg. It was not an ideal arrangement. When Brant left the US Army after his extended period of service, he wanted his wife to go back with him to America, but she refused to leave her band or her aging parents. Her husband left Britain in 1963, and she was divorced for desertion soon afterward. She never married again. When Tony Parker asked Ivy about her two failed marriages in a 1977 interview, he later said he'd expected some kind of backlash. Instead he got an honest answer: both marriages had failed because of her husbands' infidelity while she was touring. "After that, I would tell my girls, 'If you get married, don't stay in the band. For that means goodbye to romance. Take my advice and put your saxophone in the fridge.'"

Later in life when talking about her personal life, Ivy said that her first marriage had been a mistake and short-lived but that she would have liked to stay married to Brant. She used her married name Callaway as well as Benson for the rest of her life. Whether she privately regretted the choices she made or not, Ivy never said—at least not to interviewers.

14

POP GO THE BIG BANDS

Any musician trying to make a living could not ignore the explosion of different musical styles that began in the 1950s and gathered momentum throughout the 1960s. And Ivy was no exception. Although cushioned to some extent by her ongoing popularity at military bases and the resulting tours that she undertook with her band, tastes were changing, and she had to adapt. Her repertoire slowly changed from the British patriotic numbers heard on her wartime records to the more American-influenced big band style. But much bigger musical changes were ahead.

In the early 1950s, sales of American records were paramount in British popular music; 1953 saw major artists such as Perry Como, Guy Mitchell, and Frankie Laine dominating the recently introduced music charts, mostly with orchestrated sentimental ballads or novelty songs such as "(How Much Is) That Doggie in the Window?" Some wartime stars such as Vera Lynn were still popular and able to win a place on the charts, but successful new British acts such as Jimmy Young and Alma Cogan got notice with rerecorded versions of American songs. The films of the era also influenced the popularity of songs. Doris Day reached number one in 1954 with "Secret Love" from Calamity Jane and Frank Sinatra with the title song from *Three Coins in the Fountain*. A few of the big bandleaders—notably Stan Kenton in the United States and Ted Heath in the United Kingdom—continued to be successful into the 1960s but became more jazz-oriented. But many such bands had broken up after the war or were shadows of their former acts.

Musical tastes varied, however, and did not change overnight. There were, and still are, many lovers of jazz-oriented big band music. The BBC Showband featuring many jazz players featured heavily on both the Light Programme station and on television in the 1950s, and in 1964 the BBC Big Band was formed as part of a larger BBC Radio Orchestra. A standard-size big band with four trumpets, five saxophones (who doubled on other reed and wind instruments), and a rhythm section, the Big Band was used widely across BBC radio programs. In 1979, the BBC tried experimented with scheduling a twelve-part *Big Band Special* series. The Big Band became known as a jazz orchestra and grew so successful that it became a key part of radio listening. In 1994, an attempt to dismantle the BBC Big Band led to such opposition from its listening public that the BBC relented. The band, now managed outside the BBC and with freelance musicians rather than staffers, remains a key part of BBC music to this day, having continued on *Big Band Special* until the program stopped airing in 2013 and presently still appears on live broadcasts of BBC Radio 2's *Friday Night Is Music Night* and on other channels, including the BBC World Service. It is still featured in BBC 2's *Swing and Big Band Show with Clare Teal*, the successor to the *Big Band Special*, which airs on Sunday evenings. It appears regularly at the BBC Proms—an annual eight-week concert series held every summer in London and at venues across the United Kingdom—and is still considered one of the best bands in British jazz. The BBC Big Band tours, appears at festivals, and regularly records. And despite the many changes in music since the 1950s, there are still many bands playing the circuit to enthusiastic audiences.

But by the mid-1950s, the management at many performance venues would not pay for large bands; a vocalist and small group were sufficient to attract customers, and bandleaders could not afford to keep their instrumentalists on at the much higher postwar pay rates. It was still very difficult for women instrumentalists to get work. Talking to author Lucy O'Brien in 1993 for her book *She Bop: The Definitive History of Women in Rock, Pop and Soul,* Don Lusher, a trombone player with many of the big bands including Ted Heath, insisted, "We had nothing against having girls in a band . . . but you've got to remember it was a pretty high standard in those days. And maybe it wasn't as fashionable for girls then." Sheila Tracy, a trumpeter with Ivy in the late 1950s, recalled that the amount of prejudice against women was stifling. Women were savaged, she recalls: "'She looks pretty, but don't expect her to play in the same way as a man.' In my day, jazz was taboo." No wonder that women, despairing of the lack of opportunities being offered to them despite the quality of their playing, were now applying in increasing numbers to join Ivy's band.

The most significant musical change in mid-1950s Britain was the impact of American rock and roll; this provided a new impetus to performing and recording for the burgeoning youth market. At the start of the change, British popular music was dominated by American acts, or attempts to re-create American forms of music for British tastes. But soon, distinctly British forms of music began to appear, first in that uniquely British take on American jazz, blues, and folk: Skiffle, as the musical form was called, is said to have found its origins in New Orleans jazz and often featured an array of improvized instruments. It made famous artists like Lonnie Donnegan, Ken Coyer, and Chas McDevitt, but this 1950s British craze never reached much beyond Britain's shores. This was followed by the beginnings of a folk revival and then early attempts to produce an archetypal British rock-and-roll sound. Groups such as Cliff Richard and the Shadows were typical of this development, their "Move It" often cited as the first truly British rock-and-roll song.

By the late 1950s, many groups were emerging in Britain, often out of the declining skiffle scene. Most were located in major urban centers in the United Kingdom, like Liverpool, Manchester, Birmingham, and London. In Liverpool it is estimated that around 350 bands were playing in clubs, concert halls, and ballrooms at that time. The new beat groups were heavily influenced by American bands of the era, such as Texas-based band Buddy Holly and the Crickets, as well as by earlier British groups like the Shadows. And then along came the Beatles, a veritable phenomenon, who rocketed to national success in 1962, followed by other Liverpool performers, such as Gerry and the Pacemakers, Cilla Black, and the Searchers.

The taste for a new British rather than an American sound grew, and artists from Birmingham (for example, the Moody Blues), from London (the Dave Clark Five, the Kinks, and, of course, the Rolling Stones), and from Manchester (Freddie and the Dreamers) achieved rapid success. The beat movement provided most of the groups responsible for Britain's invasion of American pop charts. British rock broke through to mainstream popularity in the United States in January 1964 with the success of the Beatles' "I Want to Hold Your Hand," and they appeared in the United States on the wildly popular *Ed Sullivan Show* on February 9 of that year. The Beatles went on to become the biggest-selling rock band of all time, and they were followed by numerous British bands.

As dance bands started to die out, Ivy saw the growing influence of youth in society and the music industry, and she acted accordingly. She could not ignore the explosion of different musical styles. Ivy Benson's wartime music was definitely against the youth trend, so, always the business woman, she had to make decisions about her musical future. What would the shape of the band be in the coming years? Who would be her musicians? What kind of music would they offer? Her continuing success into the late 1950s was based on the popularity of her band among troops still serving at home and abroad, but her band diary was full with bookings at many different venues. There was still a large element of her popularity that depended on nostalgia for the spirit of a rapidly changing period of history. The band music of the 1940s was still enjoyed by a generation that had lived through the war, and her summer seasons in seaside venues in Britain were played to those whose memories of wartime and its music were still fresh.

But Ivy was nothing if not adaptable. Whilst nostalgia still held some sway, she knew that audiences were beginning to demand a wider range of musical styles. By the late 1950s, her year could include a nine-week tour to Germany to play for both troops and civilians, a concert for a teachers' conference, a thousand-mile tour of Ireland, a stint at The Ideal Home Show in Birmingham, and then a summer season on the Isle of Man, where she might play in four venues, all catering for different audiences. In 1957, one journalist commented rather disapprovingly on Ivy's inclusion of pop songs in one concert for holidaymakers: "Ivy Benson has moulded together an orchestra of infinite versatility, and her selections delighted the audience that called for repeated encores. . . . Is there some significance in the fact that the sweet melodies played by Ivy and her girls drew more demand for encores than the Rock 'n' Roll numbers?" Ivy had always given her audiences what they wanted to hear. She was a populist, not a purist, and she was prepared to include currently popular numbers in her repertoire as well as nostalgic numbers giving voice to the bygone hopes and fears of an earlier generation.

A typical program reported at that time in an Isle of Man newspaper included "A nicely varied mix of old and new hits"—"The Walls of Jericho" and "Summertime" sung by "sepia" songstress Isobel Lucas, who "stole the show." (It is jarring in our twenty-first-century world to think that "sepia" was considered an appropriate and friendly description for a black singer from Toronto). Dena Farrell, the popular soprano, sang "Oh My Beloved Father," and Toni Sharpe sang the Eartha Kitt hit "I Want to Be Evil." Sylvia Monks played solo sax in "Zambezi," a band staple at the time, and Robey Buckley, the Australian trumpeter, was said to have raised the roof. Ivy Benson herself was said to be the "life and soul of the party" and played sax and clarinet occasionally. Later in the season, the singers had mostly changed, but Dena Farrell had included as part of her set "The Lost Chord" by Arthur Sullivan (a song dating back to 1877!), which was "the highlight of the evening."

Entertainment, as many other aspects of society, went through an almost seismic shift in the Britain of the 1960s. A new, optimistic postwar generation reached adulthood in the early part of the decade. A sustained period of peace and prosperity after the long years of war and austerity indicated that what the older generation had fought and hoped for seemed to be coming to pass. The Beveridge Report of 1942—outlining the principles for eradicating poverty from Britain—and the 1944 Education Act together had laid the foundations for a healthier and more ambitious generation where birth and connections were less necessary to success than ability. *The Rise of the Meritocracy*, a novel by British sociologist and politician Michael Young, first published in 1958, was meant to be a satirical novel criticizing the tripartite system of education introduced by the Education Act. It instead became a rallying cry for the achievers, bred on notions of fairness and opportunity, who could take advantage of the seemingly unlimited possibilities.

Everything seemed to be happening at once. National Service was abolished in 1960, freeing young men to two more years of young life. Those previously denied tertiary educations by lack of finance were now supported at university by a system of grants. The country enjoyed almost full employment, and the barriers of class and accent were pushed aside in the need to fill jobs with qualified people. The idea of a fairer society seemed to become lodged in the nation's psyche as Princess Margaret married a commoner and *Lady Chatterley's Lover* was declared not to be pornographic when a scornful and amused jury was asked if they would allow their servants to read the D. H. Lawrence novel. In 1965 the death penalty was abolished, in 1966 the Race Relations Act was passed, and a grammar school boy, Edward Heath, became the leader of the Conservative Party.

And, of course, there was a loosening of the taboos on sex. In 1961, the birth-control pill became available by prescription for the first time, and in 1967 two bills, one legalizing abortion and the other homosexuality between consenting adults, reached the statute book.

Thinking back on the 1960s from a vantage point of over half a century, perhaps a picture of hippies, drugs, sex, rock and roll, and even naked revelers at music festivals come to mind. However, while the pill changed things quickly for some of that generation, particularly those in the universities and in the media and the arts, who rebelled against their parents' notion of morality, the shift in mores took much longer among ordinary young people in Britain.

And what of entertainment? In 1961, the satirical stage revue *Beyond the Fringe* opened in London, the first edition of satirical and current-affairs magazine *Private Eye* arrived on newsstands, and in 1962 the BBC ended its ban on jokes about religion, politics, sex, and royalty. They aired the new comedy program *That Was the Week That Was*, a Saturday-night "must-watch," particularly for young people.

New director-general Hugh Carleton Greene had arrived at the BBC determined to sharpen up the corporation's output. To move away from the "coziness" of existing news programs, he had put the comparatively young—at thirty-one—witty, and openly gay producer Ned Sherrin in charge of creating a live, late-night show to "prick the pomposity of public figures." The result was *TW3*, as it came to be known. Each week, the show was introduced by singer Millicent Martin belting out the theme tune, its words altered to reflect the week's news. Then a topical monologue by host David Frost, followed quickly by a series of sketches, invective from journalist Bernard Levin, songs, cartoons drawn live, monologues, and debate. It was such a departure from the usual BBC fare that of course there were a lot of complaints. Nonetheless, the BBC kept the show on for two series, only cutting it when in the run-up to the 1964 general election it was deemed appropriate for the BBC to avoid political controversy. Though never recommissioned, *TW3* inspired every satirical show that followed it. The British Broadcasting Corporation was never as cozy again. "Auntie" BBC had now become a rather naughty uncle.

According to Mark White, in *The Observers' Book of Big Bands,*

As the singers had taken over in the fifties, so by the sixties the bands had been replaced as major attractions in the States by Rock 'n' Roll ... and in England by that curiosity called the Trad Boom. This also started in the fifties with the revival of interest in traditional jazz, culminating in the enormous success of the Three B's—Chris Barber, Kenny Ball, and Acker Bilk. Economics again played a large part in all of this. The average Rock 'n' Roll or Trad Jazz group would be about five to seven musicians strong. Who needed to pay for a band of more than eighteen musicians plus a team of singers if a five- to eight-piece group would fill a theatre or a ballroom just as easily?

Ivy was an astute businesswoman. She continually reacted to the changing demand for music without losing her core base of fans. "I've got a complete library of modern music, beat music, dance music, soul music," she said, "so I judge my audiences. If I'm in a club where it's a family audience, I play family. If I'm in a place where 80 or 90 percent are teenagers, I use my head, and I play beat music and soul music."

She cut her full-scale dance band to a smaller group, varying the size to suit different bookings, and this reduction in costs enabled her to compete with pop bands and discos. Her popularity continued, and she carried on taking her band wherever she saw a good opportunity. In the early 1960s she was still visiting Hamburg for two months each winter and then entertaining US troops at Ramstein Air Force Base for a further three. She had offers to appear in Stockholm, Oslo, and Helsinki and took a group of twenty to Madrid and Majorca in the spring of 1962.

With such a hectic schedule it is not surprising that her marriage had proven difficult to sustain. Her repertoire continued to change and by this time to become quite varied depending on her audience. On one typical day that same year she and her band played for morning "Jive and Twist" sessions for teenagers at the Royal Hall in Douglas,

Isle of Man, for an Old Time Dance Festival in the afternoon, and at a midnight charity ball alongside Ronnie Aldrich and the Squadronaires, a band that had originated in the Royal Air Force and had played throughout the war.

By the end of the 1960s, Ivy and her all-women lineup was still in demand, although gone were the days of big bands. However, despite her astute business sense and willingness to adapt with the times, the signs of decline were appearing, and the bookings, while still coming in, were for less prestigious venues. "Stepping down a few leagues, like a top football team that had suffered relegation, was inevitable," writes Stephen Wade in a biographical chapter on Ivy, "which meant performing at such places as civic dances and even Masonic halls." The women players were even more likely than ever to play with the band for short periods and have other employment. Ivy rarely kept the same lineup for more than six months. The reason for losing girls remained mostly marriage, and GIs remained a great attraction, but there were increasingly more opportunities for women in the business, and the musicians moved between groups and bands.

Ivy and her band, of a size to suit whatever was required by the promoter, still spent summer seasons at the seaside. Jersey and the Isle of Man, Ivy's preferred summertime locations, were patronized by those who could afford to travel by boat or plane and were, for a time, immune from the defection of holidaymakers to cheap overseas destinations. But even such resorts were no longer what they had once been. In the 1950s and 1960s, the British seaside had enjoyed a postwar boom. Increasingly affordable to many through paid annual leave—thanks to the Holiday Pay Act 1938—families flocked to the seaside, staying in guest houses, bed-and-breakfast accommodations, hotels, or holiday camps like Butlin's or Pontins. They wanted to be entertained, and for more than twenty-five years after the war, big stars like comedian Ken Dodd and singer-comedian Des O'Connor, well-known from television appearances, spent their summers topping the bills at well-attended seaside variety shows. Even the Beatles appeared at the Winter Gardens in Margate on the Kent coast.

As the 1970s approached, however, the taste of holidaymakers for the British seaside—where they often sheltered behind windbreaks, paddled in the chilly sea, and wrapped up warmly to enjoy brass bands on the bandstand—had changed. The late 1950s and 1960s had seen cheap package holidays, combining flights and accommodation, increasing rapidly. In 1954, amendments to the Convention on International Civil Aviation allowed for a surge in mass tourism using charter planes, and people in the United Kingdom began to escape to the sun—mostly to Spain, France, and the Greek islands. And although package holidays declined somewhat by the mid 1970s, people often preferring to book flights and accommodation independently, the attraction of overseas destinations persisted, and many seaside resorts saw a continuing decline in the number of visitors and a consequent disincentive for big names in show business to consider summer seasons there.

In an interview on the island of Jersey in March 1968 with Arthur Hopcroft of the *Sunday Times*, Ivy reminisced about the 1940s and 1950s with clear memory and pleasure but without nostalgia. She insisted that dance music was a business for her. Hopcroft noted, "The girls have come and gone along with the jitterbug, jive and samba. Her music pad now has the pop world's Top Thirty, as well as the swing of early days." He was interviewing Ivy in the corner of the ballroom of the West Park Pavilion, Saint Helier, where she and the band were performing. That evening it was carnival night, and the balloons, the funny hats, and paper streamers were ready. It was a far cry from another entertainment event of 1968, the musical *Hair*, which had opened on Broadway that spring with its controversial nude, sex, and drug scenes and would open in London's West End later that year.

Ivy's girls were well-off, earning around 38 pounds per week (about 660 in today's pounds). Mostly in their late teens and early twenties, the band members were confident and not at all "girly-girly." They had cars, they had boyfriends who took them out a great deal, and they saved money. Ivy said she had no rules; after all, they were all now officially adults. But they knew what kind of behavior would cost them their jobs. She wouldn't have "any drunkenness on stage or arriving late. And they've got to be clean." Around this time, former trumpeter Sylvia Hampson, who had played with the band in the late 1940s, went to see them perform. "I didn't think the girls held her in the same reverence that we had. Times had changed."

Gone too were the days of pin-up style glamor. The stage costumes were now smart and modern. One photograph shows the band dressed in white skirts and striped blazers. The stage costume for Jersey was a light and twinkly trouser suit, and when the band was in Douglas, Isle of Man, that year, Ivy chose a woolen trouser suit, as it was so cold in the Villa Marina Gardens. Ivy dressed the band four times a year but avoided the popular miniskirts, to protect the players high on the bandstand from voyeurs. The girls were so sure of themselves, she said, and all through the year she had requests to join the band—many from girls as young as fifteen or sixteen. They alarmed her by their readiness to travel long distances on their own. She tried to persuade them to wait a bit to become professional players, unless she knew their parents or they had been recommended to her.

If the physical setting of many of the dance halls she played in had hardly changed in the thirty years she had been leading her bands— with a rotating crystal ball on the ceiling, dust motes streaming through the windows for afternoon dances, and a woodblock floor— the audiences had changed, and they varied a great deal. On one particular night, she was playing for audience members of the older generation who had come on holiday. Lady publicans and licensees from Bermondsey in London were there in a group without their husbands, and, with bouffant hairdos, wrapped in fur stoles, and fueled by drink, they invited Ivy to meet them in their hotel cocktail bar after the dance. They regarded her fondly as a much-loved celebrity and urged her to play for them. Ivy responded warmly. But, as ever in such situations, she trod "the tightrope between reserve and unseemliness." It was quite different from the previous night, when the band had played for a "beat night." Lads had danced alone, moving intricately to the music, or stood in small groups, back-combing each other's hair.

By the early 1970s, Ivy was considered enough of a celebrity to appear on BBC Radio 4's long-running program *Desert Island Discs*. She was featured on Monday, October 18, 1971, and was interviewed by host Roy Plomley. A week before her, poet and author Sir Sacheverell Sitwell, youngest of the three highly flamboyant Sitwells, had been the guest, and Ivy was followed the week afterward by the sometimes-controversial Dame of Sark. A recording reveals that Ivy's Yorkshire accent, perhaps modified for the BBC, had by now been reduced to a slight trace, although she could revert to it especially when she wanted to make a point. Naming the pieces she could not do without, she named Count Basie's "Fantail" and Benny Goodman, playing Ivy's signature tune, "Lady Be Good"—expected choices. But Aretha Franklin, Bob Dylan, and the Beatles figured, as well as Beethoven and Verdi. Her favorite track, however, was "Oh Happy Day" by the Edwin Hawkins Singers, a modern interpretation of a gospel song popular at the time. Her favorite book was *London Sparrow* by Phyllis Thompson, the second biography, recently published, of Gladys Aylward, London-born missionary to China. Perhaps Ivy had missed the first book, *The Small Woman*, in 1957, and also *The Inn of the Sixth Happiness* in 1958, a film loosely based on Aylward's life, starring Ingrid Bergman. Ivy's luxury on her imagined island? Of course—a piano.

In the summer of 1973, Ivy was on the island of Jersey with a group of ten musicians, appearing in *The Michael Bentine Show* at the Hotel de France in Saint Helier. Coincidentally, the comedian, a former member of the Goons comedy troupe, had been part of the group that had liberated the Bergen-Belsen camp in April 1945 when Ivy had been nearby and performing for his fellow airmen. But like many others who were part of that dreadful discovery, Bentine found it almost impossible to discuss.

Ivy's plans for the autumn and beyond were already well established. After the summer season she would expand the number of instrumentalists and travel to Stuttgart at the beginning of October. The band would then play a short season in Hamburg before returning to England in December. There were bookings over the winter in London and other UK venues, and the band would play a month in Bern, Switzerland. She had just received a concrete offer to play ten concerts in Hong Kong and Kuala Lumpur for the spring of 1974. "The girls all like the continental life," she said. She too enjoyed touring military bases in Germany despite repeatedly losing her band members and having to replenish the supply of women musicians. "The girls meet American servicemen who are on the US bases, fall in love, get married, and then go to make their homes in the States." Asked why she spent so much time overseas, Ivy had a simple answer: money. "You just can't get the same kind of money in England, so it's obvious that one has to go abroad, isn't it?"

Her full diary of engagements meant that she could still offer a start in the business to many young women who did not have many opportunities to play jazz professionally. Deirdre Cartwright, who recorded an album with Ivy as a teenager in 1976 and whose sister Bernice played bass guitar with Ivy for some years, said that what Ivy did was something special: While at that time there was still some discrimination in the classical music world against women performers, at least there was a structure in such music; grades, exams, and orchestras forged a path to a career and recognition in classical music. But this did not exist in jazz. Ivy offered an opportunity to belong to a professional band with high standards and an opportunity for training. However, while acknowledging the importance of Ivy Benson's band as the only professional women's band at the time providing a good source of income along with good engagements for female musicians, Cartwright found her own musical voice as a female guitarist in the second wave of feminism in the 1970s, when she started to play in a band called Jam Today and also met bassist Alison Rayner.

In the middle to late 1960s, jazz bands had become increasingly popular. Brand-new channel BBC2's *Jazz 625* program, broadcast between April 1964 and August 1966, featured performances by British and American musicians, its beginning coinciding with the end of the dispute between the UK Musician's Union and the

American Federation of Musicians. Well-known musicians—among them Duke Ellington, Dave Brubeck, Oscar Peterson, Jimmy Giuffre, Woody Herman, and Errol Garner—could now come to Britain for the first time since the 1930s, and the resurgence of jazz in Britain saw the likes of George Chisholm, Kenny Baker, Johnny Dankworth, and Tubby Hayes also performing on *Jazz 625* to large television audiences. But this expansion of the jazz scene did little to help women musicians: Although the number of men performing on the popular BBC2 program was in the hundreds, only a very few women jazz musicians appeared, and those mostly singers.

Ivy herself commented in 1971 that, although there wasn't as much prejudice against women musicians as there had once been, it was still difficult for them to get into jazz bands. She had "a girl in the band now playing wonderful jazz," she said, "and she gets so frustrated." Ivy nurtured such talent, perhaps until the times changed. Many musicians still playing jazz and who lead or have led their own bands spent time with Ivy when young: among them Claudia Lang-Colmer in the 1950s, Crissy Lee in the 1960s, Carol Gasser (née McBean) between 1966 and 1971, and Annie Whitehead in the 1970s. Annie, who joined Ivy straight out of school in 1971, and quite possibly the "talented but frustrated jazz musician," played with the band for two years. Since then she has played alongside some of the best jazz musicians and now tours her band, the Annie Whitehead Quartet, with an exciting repertoire of jazz with African influences.

In 1973, Ivy spoke of having a long waiting list to join the band. This list contained lots of guitarists, but saxophonists were hard to come by, and most of those were still recruited from the north of England. "It's musicians that I'm after, not the pretty-pretty," she said. "If I get both, then it's great, of course, but it's musicianship that comes first." In Jersey that year, she had four girls out of the ten who were officially underage, and Ivy had to take responsibility for them as their legal guardian. Young women were much more independent than they had been in Ivy's early days. "Some parents say that they feel sorry for me when their daughter is accepted for the band," she said with a laugh, "but they are a great bunch of girls." But "Don't class me as a mother-hen kind of person, though; as long as they work well, they can more or less do what they like afterwards." Things had certainly changed since the 1940s.

By the mid 1970s, Ivy's days of real success were coming to a close. The 1975 Sex Discrimination Act prohibited employers from discriminating against women. This ended the segregation of bands and allowed women to join what had previously been all-male groups. However, the same act also made it impossible for Ivy to refuse male players. She was forced to change the name of her band to Ivy Benson and Her Showband. Men did write to her asking for jobs. She said she wrote back to one of them and said the job was his—and that she hoped one of her ten to sixteen size dresses would fit him. She never heard from him again, and all her band members remained female. But by this point, her gigs were mainly private bookings and many were dependent on the nostalgia of an aging generation.

Claudia Lang-Colmer had kept in touch with Ivy and in the mid 1970s she was contacted by Ivy. "Come immediately" said the telegram. The band was playing at a holiday camp on Canvey Island and Ivy needed to replace the bass player. Claudia went to join her but found herself part of a small nine-piece orchestra and living in an awful holiday camp with cold cramped chalets. At another camp on the island, the much-reduced Eric Delaney band was playing as a quartet. Sadly, things had changed.

Ivy began to consider her future. "I certainly won't continue working until I drop," she said in 1973, "it's become a way of life, yes; but I don't want it to become a way of death." The band's appearances at nightspots and ballrooms became fewer and by 1977 she admitted to journalist Tony Parker, interviewing her after a rare appearance at a nightclub in Stockport, that she was semi-retired but hated it.

By the early 1980s, the strain of keeping the band together became too much for her and she decided to call it a day in 1982. Typical of her showmanship, she went out in style. She chose to give her final concert at the famous Savoy Hotel which has a great tradition of hosting the best of performers. In 1925, George Gershwin gave the British premiere of *Rhapsody in Blue* there; it was broadcast by the BBC, and the hotel's dance bands of the inter-war years, the Savoy Orpheans and the Savoy Havana Band, at that time described as "probably the best-known bands in Europe" played and broadcast regularly from the hotel.

Ivy Benson had confounded the many critics in the business who said that her girls could not sound as good as a man's band. And she outlasted most of the critics—and the bands.

15

SILVER LADY

In 1983, the band re-formed briefly under Ivy's baton, performing in Russell Harty's popular chat show on BBC TV to celebrate her seventieth birthday. Ivy, as slim as ever, dressed elegantly, and as usual confident in high heels, conducted as though she had never retired. Among those playing that night was Simone Smith, who had played with the band in its last years. "I'd gone from piano to just starting learning the saxophone, and I was really pushed in the deep end, and she was so strict," remembered Simone. "I'd practice for eight hours a day, and she'd come in the room and go 'No, no, no,' and she'd snatch my saxophone. She was a bit eccentric, but she taught me so much." A number of Ivy's "old girls" came to celebrate as part of the show, including Sheila Tracy, Gloria Russell, Gracie Cole, Nora Lord, and June Campbell.

And that seemed to be the last time the band would be seen. But just over a year later, in 1984, Ivy was celebrated for her long and successful career, an honor few artists achieve in their lifetime. The Birmingham Repertory Theatre produced a play *Silver Lady*, written by Liane Aukin and directed by Peter Farago, based on the lives of Ivy Benson and the women in her band. The play was billed in the program—rather ungrammatically—as "The story of Ivy Benson and her All Ladies Orchestra. The play not only pays tribute and tells the story but tries to experience for ourselves the excitement, heartache and thrill of trying something that most people would find impossible."

Ivy's band lived again. Onstage.

The playwright had spent two years carefully researching Ivy Benson's career. She had pored over old library copies of *Melody Maker* to understand the extent of the era's sex discrimination, learning that there was strict sex demarcation in the dance band era, if not always direct discrimination, and put the issue at the heart of the story. She spoke to Joe Loss, probably the longest-surviving British bandleader from the dance band era, who said that he admired Ivy but when asked if he would have a woman in his band said no. It would mean separate dressing rooms, he said, and the men wouldn't like it. His musicians were too bawdy. And this was the early 1980s!

Liane interviewed Ivy, and Peter Farago went to visit her at her home in Chiswick. By all accounts, both writer and director found it a challenge to both deal with Ivy and produce a play. Telling the life story of someone who was still very much alive and had strong opinions was not easy. Peter said that he had expected someone inspirational—a personality. But this was not obvious in the person he met. He found an ordinary woman who was happy to answer questions but one to whom he never warmed and who did not open up about her emotions. But this was Ivy; it was what she was. On stage and in the public eye, she was a performer—Ivy Benson, bandleader and celebrity, recognizable and elegant. Away from the limelight, she was private and kept her feelings to herself. Although she had spent her entire life living in close proximity to other people, she had always found it necessary to maintain a distance between herself and others. This is what had allowed her to be the leader and to make the difficult decisions that had to be made. Just a few of her "girls" became intimate friends. To most she was the respected and admired "boss."

It took *Silver Lady*'s director an unprecedented three months to assemble his cast. If the play was to work, all the female actors had to be able to play big band instruments sufficiently well to convince the audience of their authenticity. But it's one thing to secure actors who are also instrumentalists but quite another, certainly at that time, to get them to play together in simulation of a big band. Kate

Edgar—already by then well established in the music and acting profession and able to play flute, clarinet, and alto, tenor, and baritone sax—was employed as assistant musical director. She was in charge of the music onstage and also played the role of Minna in the production. She remembers starting with a raggle-taggle group of musicians, not all of whom could play the instrument required, and having to teach a trumpet player how to play the trombone. Looking back, Kate regards the production as an outstanding achievement for its time. Such a production, she thinks, would be easier nowadays when there are many more multitalented actor-musician-singers and more acting schools that train students across multiple performance disciplines.

Before rehearsals for *Silver Lady* began, Ivy spent some time with the group for photo shoots, and she attended about half of the rehearsals. She didn't rehearse the band much, but when she did, she was in her element. Ivy the bandleader and performer was back. Bossy as ever, playing the numbers on the piano and directing them in her strong Yorkshire accent—"Nay, love, not like that"—she tried to drill them into the shape of the band she had once led. One of the women commented, "I know why she's called Ivy—she drives you up the wall."

The play was in rehearsal for four weeks, and there was just one week for separately practicing the musical pieces. There were not to be many big musical numbers: the band sang an a cappella rendition of "Lady Be Good" at the end of the first act, and there were short instrumental fragments and then the finale, where the band came triumphantly together. Kate and the other actors playing band members sometimes felt threatened by Ivy's presence. Only having worked with professional musicians, Ivy could not understand the concept of actor-musicians and the process by which a play came together. She expected the actors to be able to perform music right away and was uncomplimentary—even scathing—as the actors practiced the numbers. Some of the players were terrified of her. "It was like treading on eggshells," Kate Edgar remembers. Ivy did add some suggestions as to how the band should act when playing, telling them to take charge, particularly when playing solo and to show off the instrument. "Show

how clever you are," she told them. Grudgingly, she admitted that the music improved as the show went on, and, like the audiences and the critics, she was impressed by the final number.

There is a postscript to the play that pays a tribute to the quality of the music that the actor band finally achieved. At the last-night party after the final show, everyone was dancing to what they thought was a recording of Glenn Miller's "In the Mood." Then Kate heard the sax solo and realized it was *her* solo—she was playing. The sound engineer then admitted it was a recording he had made during the show a couple of nights previously. They were all mightily impressed, Kate said.

Actor Polly Hemingway was cast as Ivy. A Yorkshire woman herself, from Bradford, and described at the time as small, slim, wide-eyed, and moving like the dancer she was, Hemingway proved ideal for the role. She had recently been very successful as Gracie Fields, the lead role in Alan Plater's play for Yorkshire Television, *The Pride of Our Alley*, and it was thought she had managed to achieve an uncanny likeness to Gracie. Although Gracie was from Rochdale in Lancashire and Ivy from Yorkshire, Polly's skill as an actress meant that, not only was she able to look like Gracie Fields and also very like Ivy Benson in her heyday, but, with a talented ear for accents, she was able to sound like them both. She was also able to identify with how Ivy would have coped with the ups and downs of performing at military bases in wartime. Her father, who would have loved to be an actor, Polly says, had told her about how he had produced shows all through the war, taking them around the military camps.

Unlike most of the other women in the cast, Polly was not a musician, and it must have been quite a challenge to find out that the part required her to play at least one number on the saxophone. Ivy helped Polly get started on the instrument, showed her how to place her mouth, and was pleased when she managed to get a sound out of the sax. According to Ivy, not many people could do that right away. Polly visited Ivy in her then home at Chiswick to get background information for her role. When she was leaving, Ivy accompanied her for a short distance. They continued to talk about how the role in the play should be handled, and Polly vividly remembers Ivy stopping in the middle of Chiswick High Road and waving her arms to demonstrate how she should conduct the band for "In the Mood," a number that featured in the play.

Silver Lady was widely reviewed. The Birmingham Rep was a major theater, and critics came not only from the Birmingham and West Midlands newspapers but also from the nationals, including the *Times* and the *Telegraph*. It was also covered by Birmingham radio station BRMB and on *Kaleidoscope*, Radio 4's arts program, presented by Natalie Wheen. Although the action of the play, especially in the first act, was criticized as jerky and disconnected, it was praised for its evocation of the era and its travails, the male chauvinism Ivy faced, and the hardships of touring. The play covered a fifty-year period, from the 1930s to the then–present day, and most critics thought that the production had caught the period flavor, the style and presentation of the band being very reminiscent of the press photos of Ivy's band in the past. Both Natalie Wheen and her interviewee, Brian Watkins from the English Department of Birmingham Polytechnic, agreed that director Peter Farago had coped very well with what seemed to them to be three plays in one: the showbiz play (but without enough music, they felt), the psychology play, and the feminist play. But they wished that the playwright had decided which play she was writing. They felt that a greater demonstration of the showbiz glitter would have helped convince the audience of the great achievement that was Ivy's career. This seemed to have been a problem also noted by other critics. Fred Norris, theater critic for the *Birmingham Evening Mail* for over fifty years, summed it up: "It is one thing finding actresses who are also accomplished musicians. It is quite another to marshal them into an orchestra and get them to swing like a Count Basie band." He said that the music sounded amateur, "And that, in every sense of the word, is what Ivy Benson and Her All-Girl band were emphatically not."

After Ivy had seen the play, she commented to Fred Norris that it had been quite an experience. "But we must do something about the music, mustn't we?" But perhaps this was inevitable. It was, after all, a play *about* Ivy Benson's band and not the real thing. As in any theatrical experience, belief has to be suspended. As the BRMB reviewer said, "It's sheer spectacle—but they wouldn't win any prizes for their playing. But still, you have to use your imagination. And the play's got a lot going for it in other ways." But for most reviewers, the music was delivered well enough to convince, and there was much praise for the final scene's big band number. For the finale, the sound of the band playing "Lady Be Good" echoed through the theater as the stage revolved to reveal the full all-girl band, dressed in golden, glittery costumes. The band then played a rousing rendition of "In the Mood." "Magnificent!" read one review. "What better finish could you ask for?"

Polly Hemingway's performance in the title role, pivotal to the play, was much praised. She was said to have worked very hard with the material she was given. This was a comment on the play rather than the actor, and phrases describing Polly's performance were extremely positive: "Polly Hemingway plays our heroine with a punchy, gritty, Northern determination." "A lively and spirited performance." "Polly Hemingway plays Ivy with vitality and warmth." Ivy herself thought that Polly looked good, "but I have been giving her a few tips," she said. "The secret, I told her, was to stand in front of the band and look sexy."

The other members of the cast who played Ivy's band were also praised as actors. But, as Brian Watkins commented on *Kaleidoscope*, it was difficult to identify the girls in the orchestra, "because they did appear, I think, as types. I could talk about the sort of silly blonde or the Liverpool Scouse or the rather vulgar Scotswoman or something; much more difficult to think of them as full parts." The writing of these parts must have been the greatest challenge for the playwright. The play covered fifty years, but there were only a handful of actors to cover the key roles. As Ivy employed hundreds and hundreds of women over that period and she rarely had the same lineup for more than six months, the development of characters who supposedly interacted over a long period could only be written as types.

Whatever the pros and cons of the production, it attracted many people who wanted to remember Ivy or were curious about who she was. Entertainment magazine *What's On* captured the play's attraction: "Whether or not you're old enough to remember the Bisto Kids, pony tails, corsets and the Princess Line—*Silver Lady* makes a marvellously nostalgic and enjoyable evening's entertainment—full of inspiration."

Ivy came onstage the first night of the show. She had arranged that she would not be playing the organ in Clacton-on-Sea, as she usually did on a Tuesday, so that she would be free to travel to Birmingham. She made a tearful, emotional appearance. Standing next to Polly Hemingway, her alter ego, her arms held an enormous bouquet of flowers while she wiped away a tear.

Retirement had continued when Ivy left her home in London and moved to Clacton-on-Sea in Essex. Her longest settled periods in life had been, since that first time in Bridlington at fifteen and excepting some periods during the war, her summer seasons at some holiday resort or another. Among the resorts she knew well were Douglas on the Isle of Man, Saint Helier in Jersey, Torquay in the southwest, and Filey in Yorkshire. She was a familiar celebrity to many who flocked to the seaside for their holidays in the postwar period. It was perhaps inevitable, then, that she chose to retire to an English seaside town—and one not too far away from London. Always a performer, she bought an organ and spent her time playing it for holidaymakers during the summer, entertaining pensioners in the winter and tirelessly raising money for charity.

Her old band members did not forget her. Some visited, and she received letters and Christmas cards from all over the world. But it seemed that appreciation of her talents would be, from then on, limited to the interest of summer visitors to Clacton and local pensioners. Occasional events reminded the public of her previous celebrity. In 1988, the polytechnic in her hometown of Leeds awarded her an honorary music degree. A *Yorkshire Post* photograph shows Ivy in gown and mortarboard in front of the polytechnic building, smiling at Sheila Tracy, one of her old band members, who holds a trombone.

Sheila was by then a well-known broadcaster, and she and Ivy were also celebrating Sheila's documentary *Lady Be Good*, which was to be premiered at the second Leeds International Film Festival held in October that year. That December 29, in the prime-time 7:35 p.m. slot, the film was shown on BBC 2. This was probably the documentary seen by teenage jazz enthusiast Clare Teal—of whom more later. Teal thought Ivy amazing and her story inspiring.

In an interview that year, Ivy admitted that, although she was happy enough with her comparatively quiet life, she sometimes felt that her life had stopped. There was the occasional reunion, and she made friends in her adopted town, but she missed her band and her life of touring. But, she said, a defiant optimist as always, "I wouldn't have wished for anything else in life. I had a million laughs. I've got enough money to live on. And I've never been frightened of being alone." Friends lobbied for her to be given a national award of some kind for her work entertaining troops, and in 1993 she was told she was to be made a dame just as Vera Lynn had been in 1975. She was delighted. But less than three months before the ceremony, Ivy died of a heart attack at age seventy-nine. Unfortunately, the honor is not bestowed posthumously. Sadly, there will never be a Dame Ivy Benson.

16

MEMORIES

Many of Ivy's former players attended her funeral. She had long been a member of the Grand Order of Lady Ratlings, an association of women in the entertainment industry, and the eulogy was given by well-known actress Ruth Madoc. Ivy's old girls spoke of the debt owed her in giving them opportunities to play as band instrumentalists at a time when it was hard for women to get such work. Many carried forward her reputation and recounted anecdotes about playing with her band when they performed in their own groups.

She wasn't forgotten in her native Yorkshire either, and from time to time articles appeared about her life in magazines and papers. Tony Parker, who had interviewed her in the 1970s, wrote an article about her life in the August/September 2004 issue of *The Yorkshire Ridings Magazine*. In 2011, a blue plaque was erected at the house she had lived in as a child—59 Cemetery Road, Holbeck, Leeds. The hospital in her adopted hometown of Clacton-on-Sea christened the Ivy Benson Ward.

But wider recognition seemed to disappear except for passing mentions in the media. In 1999, Radio 2's *Radio Days*, a series of programs recreating big band broadcasts of yesteryear, featured Ivy's theme tune, "Lady Be Good" in a program of 1940s bands. The band playing the tune was Count Basie's, but Sheila Tracy explained how popular Ivy's band had been in the 1940s and how she had adopted

"Lady Be Good" as her signature tune. At the rehearsals for the last Morecambe and Wise Christmas show in 1983, Gracie Cole, who was appearing with the duo in a comedy-music sketch, reminded them of the times that they and Ivy's band had played on the same bill over the years. Morecambe and Wise asked about Ivy and the girls and then, at the end of the show, told the audience all about Ivy and the good times they'd had together.

But the key positions in the collective public memory of great women entertainers in wartime continued to be fully occupied by Dame Vera Lynn and Gracie Fields.

Ivy Benson? Who?

But the life of Ivy still resonated with those in the theatrical profession. It is a good story: Northern girl makes good, wartime privations, glamor, up against the odds. In 2000, Gillies MacKinnon directed *The Last of the Blonde Bombshells*, a British-American television film. The script by Yorkshire-raised Alan Plater, focuses on the efforts of a recently widowed woman to reunite members of the World War II–era swing band with which she played saxophone. Set in 2000, the film is interspersed with flashbacks to the band in its wartime heyday that capture the music and atmosphere of the period. It had a stellar cast of women actors and performers: Judi Dench took the title role, along with Joan Sims, Cleo Laine, Leslie Caron, Billie Whitelaw, June Whitfield, and Olympia Dukakis, to name only a few! The British Academy of Film and Television Arts awarded Dench best actress, and the film went on to premiere in the United States on August 26, 2001, and in the United Kingdom on September 3. While not claiming to be the Ivy Benson story, the scenes set in wartime closely mirrored her band's experiences, and given the Yorkshire roots of Alan Plater, it seems almost certain that Ivy's influence on the play was strong.

Three years later, in 2004, the West Yorkshire Playhouse in Leeds premiered the performance of another of Alan Plater's scripts— *The Blonde Bombshells of 1943*. Based on the earlier film, it tells a similar story, perhaps one more closely linked to Ivy's own. Wartime bandleader Betty is in trouble. Her all-girl swing group, the Blonde Bombshells, is the greatest in the North, but it's lost half its members to illicit liaisons with American GIs. With performance on the BBC wireless imminent, the Bombshells hastily recruit new talent, including a singing nun, a hard-edged socialite, and a man who dons a woman's frock to avoid the draft.

The latter adds an amusing, imaginative, but unlikely twist to the story. Cross-dressing and the possible infiltration of a women's band by men provided an ongoing frisson, it seems. Forty-five years earlier, the American comedy film *Some Like It Hot*, in which Jack Lemmon and Tony Curtis, escaping from gangsters, dress in drag and join an all-girl touring band, had been a great success. Set in 1929, that film continues to be voted one of the best-loved comedy films of all time. Comedian Joan Shawlee played the leader of Sweet Sue and Her Society Syncopators, and Marilyn Monroe is Sugar, the band's ukulele player and vocalist and the film's romantic interest. Monroe won best actress role for her role in the film at the 1960 Golden Globe awards.

The Blonde Bombshells of 1943 was received warmly in Leeds, and audiences loved the swing music and rousing renditions of old-time favorites, such as "Don't Sit Under the Apple Tree," "T'Aint What You Do," "When I Grow Too Old to Dream," "Tweet Tweet, Shush Shush," and many more. Theater critic Michael Billington wrote in the *Guardian* of April 29, 2004, "Alan Plater's musical hits three buttons in one go: nostalgia, swing and female empowerment. With all that going for it, it's bound to have life far beyond Leeds. . . . It may not be high art, but as the song says, T'Aint What Cha Do, It's the Way That Cha Do It; and this memory-unlocking show fulfils its mission perfectly."

In 2006, Sarah Hemming, theater critic at the *Financial Times*, saw the play in London. Although slightly frustrated by the thin plot, she considered it fabulous musically. The eight key cast members were able to play the swing music as a totally convincing small band. "It is to the wartime all-girl bands," she wrote, you need to look for flair and ingenuity. Here were ladies who could cook on rations and weather German bombing raids then scrub up nicely and play the trombone with style (posh Spice take note). Alan Plater's affectionate tribute to one such band—the fictitious Blonde Bombshells—is fabulous, musically.

In Mark Babych's production, all the cast can play several instruments and do so superbly.

The description would describe Ivy's wartime band perfectly.

The play went on to entertain audiences all over the United Kingdom for the next few years; there was a national tour in 2010. And it will most likely continue to be on the list of possible productions wherever playhouses are seeking an uplifting play for their season.

Perhaps the *Financial Times*'s review mentioning the Spice Girls was read by at least one of them. Almost two decades after Ivy's death, a young woman from a generation that could never have known Ivy's band firsthand "discovered" her. On October 18, 2014, Melanie Chisholm narrated a BBC Radio 4 program on Ivy titled *Original Girl Power*. Chisholm—known as Melanie C and Sporty Spice—is a well-known solo singer, actor, songwriter, and, latterly, broadcaster, TV judge, and charity worker. She was for some years in the mid 1990s, and briefly when they re-formed for a tour from 2007 to 2008, a member of the Spice Girls, the best-selling female group of all time. Assembled to exploit the girl-power phenomenon of the 1990s, the Spice Girls were popular cultural icons of that time. Melanie was surprised at what she found when learning Ivy's story. She admitted that she hadn't heard of Ivy until then, "which is incredible, considering what a trailblazer she was." Melanie was puzzled as to why Ivy's fame had waned and was eager to introduce her to new audiences through the BBC documentary. "I find it incredibly inspiring to hear of Ivy's story," she said.

The documentary interviews many former members of Ivy's band, among them Sylvia Hampson, Margaret Roe, and Gloria Russell, all of whom played or sang with Ivy in the immediate postwar years.

Chisholm was fascinated with what she heard: "It was Ivy's passion and talent that paved the way for the Spice Girls. There's no doubt in my mind that in musical terms Ivy Benson was the originator of girl power. The Spice Girls may be the band most closely associated with girl power, but Ivy pioneered it."

The program was reprised on Radio 4 Extra on March 7, 2015. Listeners who had missed the first airing were thus prepared for the second program Chisholm presented on Ivy: *Sax Appeal: Ivy Benson's All Girl Band*, which aired two days later. It continues Ivy's story into the postwar period, recounting a number of stories from Ivy's old band members from that period, including Joyce Clark (née Terry) and Gloria Russell, who both sang with the band, and June Smith, Margaret Chappell, Sylvia England, and Patsy O'Hara, who were all instrumentalists. Interest in the Benson band was rekindled.

The swing and jazz music of the big bands has enjoyed something of resurgence since the millennium, with the formation of many smaller jazz-focused bands. Jazz has increasingly been heard at the Proms, a program once limited to classical music. The year 2014 saw the Proms' first Battle of the Big Bands, presented by Clare Teal, well-known jazz singer, bandleader, and broadcaster. Since then, the Albert Hall Big Band Prom concert has been a much-appreciated highlight of the season. In 2017, Clare presented the Guy Barker and Winston Rollins big bands, there to celebrate the triumphs of big band greats, including Duke Ellington, Count Basie, Benny Goodman, Tommy Dorsey, Jimmie Lunceford, Boyd Raeburn, Machito, Stan Kenton, and Woody Herman.

Perhaps Ivy's band, at least reduced in size as it was in its later days, would not be seen as a band to compete with the likes of Count Basie's and Tommy Dorsey's, but it is still remembered as something special. In autumn 2014, a concert was held in Bristol at Future Inn in celebration of the centenary of Ivy's birth—late 2013. The special anniversary tribute featured music from four surviving members of the band, among them Claudia Lang-Colmer (double bass), who worked with Ivy and toured with her across Europe for a number of years.

Like many others who had played with Ivy throughout the late 1950s to the 1970s when, unlike in wartime, women had more choices of work, Lang-Colmer still remembered Ivy as pivotal to her professional choices. "My career wouldn't be where it is without Ivy," she told an interviewer. "She was a wonderfully charismatic woman and a truly historic figure who set the mould for classic dance band jazz—the kind that appears in the Great American Songbook. Ivy was unique and such a determined, glamorous person. She really stood up for women."

On April 8, 2015, three of Ivy's "old girls" met up at the Vortex Jazz Club in North London as the Ivy Benson Reunion Band: Carol Gasser (née McBean), Claudia Lang-Colmer, and Crissy Lee. Although not strictly a reunion, as the women had never previously played together in Ivy's band, the gig was a tribute to her. And in February 2018, the reunion band, now with just two of Ivy's players, Claudia Lang-Colmer and Chrissy Lee, played once again at the club.

17

LEGACY

When in 2017 I bought a CD of great British dance bands, I fully expected to find Ivy's band there. After all, the collection included many of her fellow bandleaders, including Jack Hylton, Henry Hall, Victor Silvester, and Billy Cotton. It even had a track by a woman bandleader, Mrs. Jack Hylton, who had led a short-lived and little-remembered band in the mid 1930s. I was disappointed. Maybe the omission was because Ivy did not record much in the early 1940s. Nevertheless, a band that was routinely at the top of the popularity lists on ENSA tours for many years and known as the Forces' Sweetheart Band surely deserved to feature.

I looked elsewhere for her to figure alongside the other dance band greats. I met with little success. Even in *The Observers' Book of Big Bands*, in which Mark White wrote about over fifty dance bands of the 1920s onward, there was no mention, even as a passing reference, of Ivy. *Dancing around Britain* by Len Goodman contains a list of forty-three dance bands with their theme songs. Only one band led by a woman is mentioned—Ina Ray Hutton and Her Orchestra. No mention of Ivy Benson or of "Lady Be Good."

Most of the coverage of her band is in books by women—notably, those by Sheila Tracy (*Talking Swing*) and Lucy O'Brien (*She Bop*), who had either worked with Ivy or recognized her contribution to wartime entertainment. They highlighted her unique success as a woman bandleader for over forty years, coping within a chauvinistic environment. But the authors were also very keen to emphasize that, as a woman in the music business, Ivy insisted on excellent musicianship among her players.

Perhaps the continuing lack of male recognition was because many of the surviving bands postwar tended to become more jazz-oriented and there were more men than women recognised as jazz musicians at that time. Ivy's instrumentalists could play jazz with the best of them—many going on to play or lead well-respected jazz groups and bands. But as the years went on, her repertoire was necessarily more mixed. She played popular music to meet the demands of her changing audiences. Not all those who worked for her were comfortable with what they were asked to play; recall the story in an earlier chapter of one of her players who challenged Ivy's authority, tearing up her music and refusing to play German drinking songs she considered "not proper music." However, without such flexibility of repertoire, Ivy would not have survived. And above all else, she wanted to remain successful in the business.

The fact remains, however, that despite creating a big band that was on a par with the major male bands of the day and despite blazing a trail for excellence in her musicians at a time when, she said, "the weaker sex were [sic] not expected to play anything stronger than a parlour violin," Ivy Benson is remembered as a novelty. She is thought of by many as a woman bandleader who led an all-women band rather than as a professional who insisted on musical excellence. However, without exception, all those who worked with her speak about her belief in the quality of her music. They describe how she insisted that her musicians play music to equal that of the other, mostly male, bands. She was a hard taskmaster.

Latterly, she has been recognized as a feminist icon, a role that she acquired incidentally by continuing to fight for the success of her band against a lot of male prejudice. It is unlikely, when she started out as a bandleader in 1939, that her main intention was to widen the boundaries of female emancipation. The role of someone who stood up for women in her profession was thrust upon her by history and circumstance. As an individual, however, Ivy Benson knew she was as talented as any man, and she wanted to be recognized for it.

The more she worked with women, the more convinced she was that they were men's equals in musical ability, and the more frustrated and determined she became when this was denied. When World War II began, there was an increased need for entertainment both for the troops and for civilians to maintain morale and at the same time a shortage of male instrumentalists. Bands were decimated as men were called up to military service and women and older male instrumentalists were suddenly in demand. Ivy took full advantage of the situation and decided on a band format that served her well for the ensuing years. She was lucky too in being able to start her all-ladies band with an almost full lineup, thanks to a fortunate, for her, situation: Twelve fellow instrumentalists dissatisfied with their jobs playing for the overstretched and ailing Teddy Joyce persuaded Ivy to start a band and threw in their lot with her.

Ivy had not expected the chauvinism she found in the industry. Once established, she constantly battled for musical quality of her band to be recognized and for fair pay. This turned her into a fighter for women and ignited in her a desire for her band to be considered alongside the best. "She really fought for us," says Claudia Lang-Colmer. Many of those who worked for her became imbued with the same fighting spirit. Ivy insisted on hiring the best instrumentalists or sought out those with the most promising potential. She trained and coached them intensely, disciplined them tightly with regard to their music, and always maintained high expectations. Ivy criticized the band if "they sounded like women," and she was determined that "only being women" could not be used as an excuse for belittling her band.

And yet it often was.

However, Ivy never thought running a women's band required the same approach as leading a band made up of men, and she had mixed views about it. To be sure, she fought hard to be recognized as an equal with the bandleaders of her era and won many gender battles.

But she was also critical of what she saw as a negative female attitude to musicianship that she claimed to perceive in women as opposed to men. Even in 1971, when the feminist movement was well established, she could say that although she thought that the sound of women in a band was no different than an all-male lineup, women "have naturally not got the stamina of men. They're not built that way, are they?" I suspect that any woman instrumentalist these days would scoff at that remark. When was the last time you saw a woman jazz player leaving her male colleagues on stage to go rest because she lacks stamina?

Ivy thought women's emotions got in the way of their professionalism at times—a problem she did not see in men. Of course, she never led an all-male band and could not be aware of any factors that caused similar emotional problems in such bands, except by hearsay. And although she was an excellent musical coach for women instrumentalists, there is not much evidence that she coached them in band-leading skills—at least, not with a view to planning for succession. There is no real evidence that, apart from periods of illness when she was obliged to relinquish her baton, she saw anyone among her musicians who might eventually follow her, except for maybe Robey Buckley. Ivy's attitudes were those of her generation rather than those of later, more-emancipated women. "Men have a job to do and usually a wife and family to keep. A girl's commitment was not always as strong," she reminisced toward the end of her life as a bandleader. "If [one of her players] had a boyfriend, he only had to say, 'Either you stay with me or we're through,' and I had another empty chair."

And although when interviewed during her career, she usually claimed that she didn't have much trouble running an all-woman band, except in losing her players to marriage and pregnancy; in retirement she admitted that there had been some other problems. She had advised her girls on how to cope with the unwanted pregnancies that occurred from time to time, had cared for one woman who had a drinking problem, and said that menstrual cycles sometimes meant that players felt unable to perform. The script of *Silver Lady* includes the line, "Her Tony is out in France, fighting for our survival, and I can't even keep a scrappy, grumbling, grousing, self-centred, limping band of women together." The line is made up, but it did represent Ivy's occasional frustrations with her touring band, and she had shared her views in interviews with the playwright.

Her choice of an all-women lineup at the start of her career was partly influenced by wartime opportunities and constraints, as well as her determination to succeed as a woman in a hostile male environment. Giving opportunities to many women who would not otherwise have played professionally was a by-product of her personal ambition. Ivy had an indomitable spirit and such an urge to succeed that, as one critic put it after seeing *Silver Lady*, "you get the impression that the girls are so much fodder to feed Ivy's ego." This may be an extreme view and emphasized by the playwright for dramatic purposes, but it is true that at the beginning of her career Ivy was more personally involved with her players and felt let down when one of them left the band. Later she became more detached, more philosophical about losing musicians, and her primary concern became the need to maintain the lineup she required. The play also attributes to Ivy the line, "I want guts, not tits. I want glamour, not sex. I want first-class players. I want a decent wage." This was certainly an Ivy sentiment, and all her efforts were focused toward this goal.

It turned out that with her all-girl band Ivy had created a good format—attractive young women playing music people wanted to hear. In wartime, glamor was in short supply, and there were many lonely young men missing wives and girlfriends. A beautifully dressed group of girls playing swing, but also performing heartfelt ballads of separation and longing, was bound to be a success. Her decision in the postwar period to keep an all-women lineup seems to have been based on her recognition that she had established a good business model that would probably continue to work for her. And it did work well, for many years. She took the opportunity from 1945 onward to tour military bases in Europe and further afield, as well as working extensively in the United Kingdom and beyond for civilian gigs. Her fame, pervasive wartime nostalgia in postwar Britain, and her willingness to keep up-to-date and give customers what they wanted ensured her survival long after more conventional bands had disappeared from the scene. And despite equality legislation in the 1970s, she never employed a man.

There is no doubt that Ivy did influence women musicians and increased their confidence in moving forward in their careers—particularly those who were real jazz musicians and who struggled for recognition, despite the big strides women were then making in other popular-music genres. Deirdre Cartwright, interviewed in 2004, recalled how some of the bigger women's bands in the 1970s were modeled a bit on Ivy and on the band members' memories of working with her. Lydia D'Ustebyn's Ladies Swing Orchestra, in which Deirdre played, and which also contained ex-Benson member Annie Whitehead, was a rather tongue-in-cheek feminist swing band of all-female musicians. Lydia D'Ustebyn was not a real person but a fictional character based on Ivy Benson. The band would frequently joke that Lydia was absent from performances because she had "missed the train." This was part of the fun. Ivy, of course, was so extremely organized that she would never have missed any train.

In some ways, the emergence of women in jazz and dance bands lagged behind their appearance in rock bands. The late 1960s and 1970s saw a bewildering increase in the number of women who played guitar, drums, and keyboard in rock, soul rock, and punk bands or who fronted the bands on vocals. In the 1960s, all-girl rock groups such as the United Kingdom's Liverbirds played in Germany with the same success as the Beatles, and in the United States Janis Joplin fronted bands with a swagger and with an attitude toward male-female relationships, drugs, and sexuality new to the music business.

Women musicians seemed to be emerging all the time in the 1970s and 1980s, all across musical genres, but particularly in rock and punk. The Runaways in the United States, the punk band the Slits, and punk-metal Girlschool had or still have all-female lineups, and women started bands and fronted many others. Elkie Brooks with Vinegar Joe, the androgynous-looking Patti Smith, and Chrissie Hynde—who founded her own band, the Pretenders in 1978—changed the look of women in bands forever. These were rock bands that, like Ivy's in her early days, wanted to attract audiences primarily with the quality of their music. But unlike Ivy's musicians, these women were in no way intentionally glamorous. They were tough and increasingly breaking away from controlling male management. They dressed how they wanted to and aimed to live their lives uninhibited by gender stereotypes.

Many of the women in early rock groups were growing up in the 1960s when attitudes toward sex, gender, and class were changing rapidly. The 1970s saw the rise of feminism, which brought about a change of attitude toward women in all walks of life. Feminist politics coming from America in the 1970s led to campaign groups and conferences all over the United Kingdom, and these would often book all-women bands. While some of these were rock and punk groups, bigger bands with a jazz component were also in demand. To put such a band on stage at that time was in itself a political act, according to Deirdre Cartwright.

All-women bands such as the Sisterhood of Spit, a twenty-two- to twenty-four-piece all-women dance band, and Jam Today were big bands that consciously chose an all-women format. There was no place for men in them. Jam Today, started by Alison Rayner, took responsibility for setting up their own equipment and providing their own sound engineers. Like other women leading bands in the 1970s, Rayner thought it important that they create their own style and not just subscribe to the male-dominated music of the time. Typically, the choice of name was apt. Her band was named after the White Queen's nonsensical rule in *Through the Looking Glass*: "The rule is, jam tomorrow and jam yesterday—but never jam today." Alison was uninterested in conformity: "And we thought, no—we want jam today." Jam Today and similar groups were entirely different from Ivy's band. There were no defined individual leaders, although inevitably there had to be leadership where necessary. These were groups of strong women choosing to work with other strong women.

But the bigger, male-led, and jazz-focused bands were still much less mixed than classical orchestras; the ad hoc lifestyle of men in some jazz bands, the hanging around, and the way gigs were won meant that women tended to lose out. Some of the old members of Ivy's band joined their younger "sisters" in the 1980s to play jazz. One of them, Gracie Cole, met and played trumpet with musicians fostered by the women's movement. As there were few commercially viable large ensembles at that time, rehearsal bands in which session musicians played jazz for pleasure became Gracie's natural home. And the enthusiasm of the younger women she played with made her reassess her own pioneering role and that of Ivy and those who had blazed an early trail for female instrumentalists in bands. Gracie gave interviews and welcomed the attention. And Simone Smith, only in her twenties when playing with Ivy in the Russell Harty show, went on to be a founding member of the successful Five Star Swing, a band that still specializes in swing and big band music and plays sounds from the 1940s onward. Despite the seismic shifts in popular music since World War II, there is still a taste for swing among those who can never have seen or heard the original bands live.

By the mid 1990s, opportunities for women had changed considerably. Clare Teal, another woman from Yorkshire—born in the village of Kildwick in 1973—was entering the music profession. Probably the most successful jazz and swing singer and big band leader of her generation, Clare had heard her father playing her grandma's collection of big band records from an early age and was strongly influenced by the likes of Ella Fitzgerald, Billie Holliday, and Joe Loss. Clare was also impressed by the story of Ivy Benson, which she had heard on a radio program in her early teens. She thought Ivy amazing. In many ways, Clare's success story parallels that of the young Ivy: She retains a strong awareness of her Yorkshire heritage, and despite living elsewhere for many years she still feels like a Northerner. She is "never not from Yorkshire," as she says.

And just like Ivy, the same early ability, opportunity, luck, and drive all played key roles in Clare's success. Called for an unexpected music examination while at university, she realized she had forgotten her clarinet and so sang instead. She got her "best grades ever" and found she enjoyed singing in public. Mixing a full-time job in advertising with singing with bands in her spare time, her big chance came when she was asked to stand in for American jazz singer Stacey Kent at a festival in Llandrindod Wells. With such an accolade behind her and a strong determination to succeed, Clare then used her savvy and self-promotion to win a three-record contract with Candid Records. Her popularity soared with appearances on radio and television, and in 2004 she released her first album for Sony Jazz in what was then the biggest recording deal by any British jazz singer. However, unlike Ivy, who had little personal support throughout her career except from her father, Clare says that she and her partner, Muddy Field, embarked on a journey into the unknown together and that "although we were ripped off a bit in the early days, starting from a position of absolute cluelessness, we learned as we went along, working alongside wonderful and generous people."

When asked whether she had ever encountered any prejudice as a woman who not only sings but leads lots of different ensembles—such as Trio, Big Mini Big Band, Big Band, and Hollywood Orchestra—Clare reflects, "On the whole, I have never suffered any negative reactions as a female bandleader, apart from a one-off occasion where a gentleman who had booked us for a concert refused to present the fee cheque to me and insisted on passing it instead to a male backing vocalist." She is thrilled that she is meeting more and more talented young female musicians and singers who are writing their own arrangements, leading their own ensembles, and progressing in the same way as their male counterparts. Most of the bands she works with have women playing in them, and in all the ensembles and bands she leads, male and female players are selected for both their ability and positive attitude with no reference to gender.

Moving into the third decade of the twenty-first century, female and male musicians work alongside each other and compete for the same jobs. The concept of women's roles and men's roles is fast disappearing. Women now usually take their place without comment alongside men in mixed lineups. The argument as to whether women make good instrumentalists is redundant. Some of our best saxophonists, clarinettists, and trumpeters are women and recognized for their professionalism. But it isn't all perfect. We have a long way to go before we can call women's treatment equal. The gender gap in pay in the entertainment industry is still one of the largest when compared with other professions. While writing this chapter of the book, I noticed in the morning paper that one all-women group had sacked their agent upon finding that their male equivalents playing at a festival were being paid ten times more. And women instrumentalists report that some men in groups still resist having women join and comment unfavorably.

But there is no question that there are now many more women like Ivy Benson—women who do not doubt their abilities, are perfectly capable of leading their own bands, and want the best, gender being a nonissue. As Clare Teal comments, "Ivy should be remembered for the great work she did, and it is our duty to carry Ivy's message of equality forward to future generations so that we don't have a need for all-male or all-female bands—just bands of great musicians working together to make amazing music that makes everyone listening feel fantastic."

There is, admittedly, a generation of young musicians who never knew Ivy Benson and may not even recognize her name. But if they were to look closely at the history of women's success in band music, they would find that name frequently present. It is there, signaling the ability of a woman to succeed and fight for that success in what was once a very male-dominated part of the music business. But more than that, it is the name of a woman who encouraged, coached, and instilled confidence in many women musicians who followed her. She gave them chances to perform and hone their skills in a professional band environment when such chances were hard to come by.

The name of Ivy Benson resounds through the history of band music.

ACKNOWLEDGMENTS

Without a great deal of help and support, biographies can never be written. While working on this book I have been aided by many people who have given me their thoughts, opinions, and information about Ivy Benson, her life and times, and band music and the role of women in such music. Clare Teal, jazz singer and bandleader, has been extremely helpful, as have stage director Peter Farago and musical director Kate Edgar. Polly Hemingway gave me insight into playing Ivy and gave me access to her collection of reviews for *Silver Lady*. Claudia Colmer-Lang generously shared with me her experiences working with Ivy, and through his essay on his grandmother Nora Coward (née Lord) and subsequent correspondence, James Ure gave me additional insights into band life in the 1950s.

Others have helped me access information, often going out of their way to point me in the right direction—to the people, archives, or illustrations that I needed. For these things I have to thank particularly Belinda Biggins, assistant to Clare Teal; Deirdre Cartwright, jazz musician; Helen Skilbeck at Leeds Central Library, Leeds Civic Trust; Marco Campanini in the Reference and Local Studies department in Saint Helier, Jersey; and Sue Deeley, who arranged permissions from the Birmingham Repertory Theatre. Sarah Christian in the Isle of Man library in Douglas has been a very special help, smoothly arranging access to articles and photographs.

My editor Carol Flannery has kindly, patiently, and efficiently guided me throughout the publishing process; the team at Rowman has been a pleasure to work with.

Kirsty, Anna, and Olivia, my daughters, have encouraged me in the writing of the book, offering the views of younger women. And it goes almost without saying that my partner, Keith Alldritt, has been endlessly supportive, urging me forward and helping me think through the inevitable problems of writing such a story.

Many thanks to you all.

BIBLIOGRAPHY AND SOURCES

Army Bureau of Current Affairs, [British]. *Yanks: British Views on America during the Second World War.* Compilation. [Ireland]: Books Ulster, [1941–1945] 2016.

Atkins, Kate. Interview by Janet Tennant. Discussion with the musical director and actress in *The Silver Lady*, play by Liane Aukin, debuted at the Birmingham Repertory Theatre, 1984. Salisbury, Wiltshire. July 19, 2018.

Baade, Christine L. *Victory through Harmony: The BBC and Popular Music in World War II.* Oxford and New York: Oxford University Press, 2012.

Beale, Kathleen Jessie. "Beale, Kathleen Jessie (Oral History)." Catalogue number 10775. Interview in three parts. Lyn E. Smith, recorder. Imperial War Museum. June 13, 1989. https://www.iwm .org.uk/collections/item/object/80010552.

Benson, Ivy. "Benson, Ivy (Oral History)." Catalogue number10630. Interview in three parts. Grieg Miles, recorder. Imperial War Museum. March 3, 1989. https://www.iwm.org.uk/collections/ item/object/80010408.

Billington, Michael. Review for *Blonde Bombshells of 1943* at the West Yorkshire Playhouse, Leeds. *Guardian*, April 29, 2004. https:// www.theguardian.com/stage/2004/apr/29/theatre.

Bradford, Eveleigh. "They Lived in Leeds: Ivy Benson (1913– 1933) and Her All Girls Band." Life and Style. *North Leeds Life Magazine*, February 2015: 8. https://issuu.com/northleedslife /docs/2015_feb_a.

Bret, David. *The Real Gracie Fields: The Authorized Biography*. London: JR Books, 2010.

Brown, Reginald. "Leader in a League of Her Own." *Yorkshire Post*, May 7, 1993: 15. Reflections on career of Ivy Benson.

Colmer-Lang, Claudia. Interview by Janet Tennant. Discussion with double bass player who performed with Ivy Benson, 1954–1962. Telephone. August 2, 2019.

Connolly, Ray, ed. *In the Sixties*. London: Pavilion Books Ltd., 1995.

Farago, Peter. Interview by Janet Tennant. Discussion with the director of *The Silver Lady*, play by Liane Aukin, debuted at the Birmingham Repertory Theatre, 1984. London. September 20, 2018.

Goodman, Len. *Dancing around Britain*. Liverpool: Trinity Mirror Media, 2014.

Hemming, Sarah. Review for *Blonde Bombshell of 1943*, London. *Financial Times*, July 25, 2006. https://www.ft.com/content/ee2d191e-1bf0-11db-a555-0000779e2340.

———. "The Great Gracie Cole: My Story." 4barsrest.com. April 14, 2005. https://www.4barsrest.com/articles/2005/art464.asp.

Hemingway, Polly. Interview by Janet Tennant. Discussion of Ivy Benson as portrayed in *The Silver Lady*, play by Liane Aukin, debuted at the Birmingham Repertory Theatre, 1984. London. June 13, 2018.

Horn, Adrian. *Juke Box Britain: Americanisation and Youth Culture, 1945–60*. Manchester: Manchester University Press, 2009.

McKay, George. *Circular Breathing: The Cultural Politics of Jazz in Britain*. Durham, N.C.: Duke University Press, 2005.

Merriman, Andy. *Greasepaint and Cordite: How ENSA Entertained the Troops during World War II*. London: Aurum, 2013.

Nicholson, Virginia. *Perfect Wives in Ideal Homes: The Story of Women in the 1950s*. London: Penguin Books, 2016.

O'Brien, Lucy. *She Bop: The Definitive History of Women in Rock, Pop and Soul*. London: Penguin Books, 1995.

Parker, Tony. "The Band Leader Who Invented Sax Appeal." *Yorkshire Ridings Magazine* (August/September 2004): 35.

Parsonage, Catherine, and Kathy Dyson. "A Brief History of British Women Jazz Players." Commissioned by Fondazione Adkins Chiti: Donne in Musica, 2007. Available online at http://www.chrishodgkins.co.uk/wp-content/uploads/2017/08/Britain-Jazz-Women.-Dr-Catherine-Parsonage-and-Dr-Kathy-Dyson.pdf.

Ravenhill, Brian. http://www.ivybenson-online.co.uk/biographies/1bio_data.htm (website defunct). The information previously held on this 2005 website is now lodged with The Jazz Heritage Wales as part of a donation by Brian Ravenhill in 2010. The archive contains the contents of website http://www.ivybenson-online.co.uk, plus oral histories from members of the Ivy Benson Orchestra, correspondence, papers, and VHS and DVD recordings. Contact jazzheritage@uwtsd.ac.uk or Dylan Thomas Centre, Somerset Place, Swansea, SA1 1RR, UK.

Rosenthal, Jack. *Letters from an Airfield: The True Story of a GI Bride of the Mighty Eighth*. Stroud, England: History Press, 2009.

Smith, Albert Hugh. *The Place-Names of the West Riding of Yorkshire*. English Place-Name Society, 8 vols. Cambridge: Cambridge University Press, 1961–1963.

Silver Lady Collection. Wolfson Centre for Archival Research, Birmingham Central Library. MS 2239/1/304: MS 2239/1/304/1, MS 2239/1/304/3, MS 2239/1/304/4, MS 2239/1/304/6, MS 2239/1/304/7, and MS 2239/1/3048. http://calmview.birmingham.gov.uk/CalmView/Overview.aspx.

Teal, Clare. Interview by Janet Tennant. Discussion with the jazz singer, bandleader, and broadcaster. E-mail. August 3, 2018.

Tracy, Sheila. *Talking Swing: The British Big Bands*. Edinburgh: Mainstream, 2008.

Tucker, Sherrie. *Swing Shift: "All-Girl" Bands of the 1940s*. Durham, N.C.: Duke University Press, 2000.

Ure, James. "To What Extent Were the Musical Performances of Ivy Benson's All-Girl Band Influenced by Their Social Context?" Undergraduate extended essay, University of Huddersfield, Huddersfield, West Yorkshire, England, 2017.

Wade, Stephen. "Queen of the All Girls Band." In *Heroes, Villains and Victims of Leeds*, 159–63. Derby, Eng.: Breedon Books, 2007.

White, Mark. *The Observers' Book of Big Bands.* The Observers' Pocket Series, vol. 77. London: Frederick Warne, 1978.

Wordsworth, Clair, prod. *Ivy Benson: Original Girl Power.* Melanie Chisholm, presenter. Sue Clark Productions. BBC Radio 4. October 18, 2014. https://www.bbc.co.uk/sounds/play/b04lp3x7.

————, prod. *Sax Appeal: Ivy Benson's All Girl Band.* Melanie Chisholm, presenter. Sue Clark Productions. BBC Radio 2. March 9, 2015.

Young, Michael. *The Rise of the Meritocracy.* London: Thames and Hudson, 1958.

Yorkshire Post. "In Harmony." October 18, 1988. Front page. Honorary degree presentation to Ivy Benson by Leeds Polytechnic.

————. "Leeds Nostalgia: Leeds Women Who Changed the World." June 24, 2016. https://www.yorkshireeveningpost.co.uk/news/leeds-nostalgia-leeds-women-who-changed-world-618002.

INDEX

ABOUT THE AUTHOR

Born in Lancashire in the north of England, **Janet Tennant** spent many years lecturing and training in management, traveling throughout Europe and beyond. She worked in private companies, public organizations, and charities to study and improve workplace relationships. Meeting so many people, she knows that there is a unique story in everyone's life and that many factors affect what we become. Enjoying the arts, particularly theater, opera, and music, as well as having been an enthusiastic but very amateur actress, she enjoys writing about those in the arts. Her last book, *Mistress and Muse*, highly acclaimed by music critics, tells the story of Ursula, poet, librettist, and lover of composer Ralph Vaughan Williams. Tennant now lives in the Midlands of England with her partner, the writer Keith Alldritt. She has three daughters and a son.

PHOTO CREDITS